SNEAK IT THROUGH

SNEAK IT THROUGH

SMUGGLING MADE EASIER

MICHAEL CONNOR

PALADIN PRESS
BOULDER, COLORADO

Sneak It Through:
Smuggling Made Easier
by Michael Connor

Copyright © 1984 by Michael Connor

ISBN 0-87364-282-1
Printed in the United States of America

Published by Paladin Press, a division of
Paladin Enterprises, Inc., P.O. Box 1307,
Boulder, Colorado 80306, USA.
(303) 443-7250

Direct inquiries and/or orders to the above address.

Illustrations by Bill Border

CONTENTS

FOREWORD

SNEAK IT THROUGH SUGGESTS many useful places of concealment applicable to a wide range of covert import-export situations and describes methods and tactics that will give you a definite advantage when the going gets tough.

Ingenuity is the key word. By adapting these methods to suit specific requirements, a higher success rate can be expected.

1.
PLACES OF CONCEALMENT

Many of the stashes detailed in this chapter are especially suitable for borders and checkpoints that allow free access to citizens passing back and forth, and for so-called secure areas. For example, in Belfast, Northern Ireland, certain shopping centers designated as secure areas are effectively enclosed by checkpoints to deter the transportation of unauthorized and illegal items, usually explosives. (The secure areas of Northern Ireland also serve to restrict the movement of certain persons, but that's a different story.)

Although a cursory search can be expected at such borders and checkpoints, the volume of traffic prevents the thorough examination of all but the most suspicious persons and vehicles. The obvious exception to this rule is the spot check, in which any poor sod is picked out at random and given the full treatment. However, once you have read *Duty-Free* and *Sneak It Through,* a search of any type should not give you cause for concern.

The usual search will include a mirror check on the underside of the vehicle, which will reveal poorly hidden items, examination of the engine and truck compartments, maybe a glance into the glovebox, and a quick check of hand baggage. Some form of magnetometer screen will probably be employed to detect possible metallic objects concealed on the traveler's person, and a "sniffer"—electronic or canine— may also be used to determine whether drugs or explosives are present.

Adopting the cover of a tradesman, such as a painter, plumber, or builder, can open a great many doors by providing the justification for carrying a variety of trade-related implements and tools which can be adapted to conceal goods.

Cans of paint, creosote, and other liquids make excellent hides, as it is most unlikely that guards or officials will examine them except to remove the lid and confirm that they contain the relevant substance. Thick, heavy liquids, such as the jelly type of non-drip paint or vehicle rustproofing material, are recommended. Detection of items hidden in these materials is not as easy as with thin fluids, which lend themselves to a dipper stick test. Always make sure that the items are well protected from the fluid (sealing in plastic bags is effective) and that the contents of the can cover the contraband sufficiently. The dirtier and messier the cans the better, as messiness will often deter close examination.

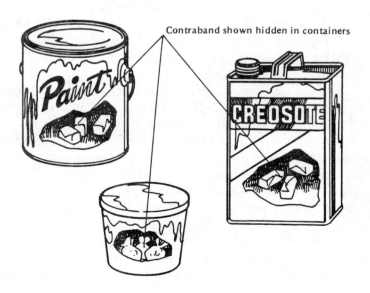

Contraband shown hidden in containers

Ladders, used in a variety of trades, can be readily adapted to create space for contraband, and in many cases the available space is considerable. Most ladders are made of either wood or aluminum. If you use the aluminum type, all the hard work is done for you, as they are of a tubular construction which allows items to be inserted into the rails through existing openings at the top and bottom. Sometimes the ends of the rails are sealed or bent over, but in most cases it will be a simple matter to remove the plug or bend open the end piece. Once the contraband is in place, reseal the opening and doctor the ladder to give the impression of age and wear. If you are in a hurry, items may also be hidden in the hollow rungs of the ladder, but obviously this method is not as safe. Plug the openings with plastic car body-filler, wooden or metal stops, clay, or mud.

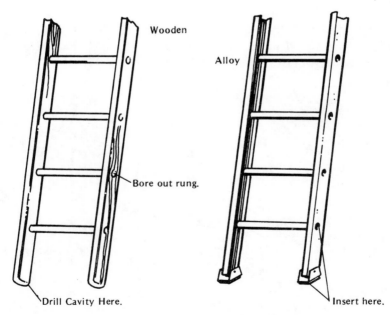

Wooden ladders can be disassembled according to their construction, and cavities drilled in the rails or rungs. Take care not to weaken the ladder too much, as it may well be thrown to the ground during a search of the vehicle. Bore out hides with a large drill bit, insert items and reassemble the ladder. Seal the holes with plastic filler and add a coat of paint as a finishing touch.

Large-handled tools like spades, forks, and brooms can be treated in a similar fashion, with excellent results.

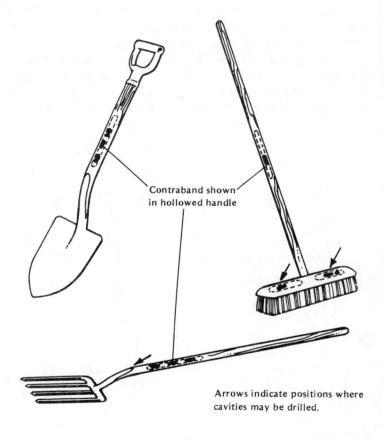

Contraband shown in hollowed handle

Arrows indicate positions where cavities may be drilled.

Another excellent stash well adapted to the tradesman cover is that of the house brick—or rather several dozen of them! Cast your own special bricks by constructing a wooden mold modelled on a genuine brick; then pour in plaster or cement. The items to be transported must be well sealed in suitable material to protect them from the cement, which will eat through certain materials, such as fabric. If plastic is used as a sealer, use at least a six-mil thickness, such as heavy-duty trash bags. Remember also that both plaster and cement heat up as they dry. If your contraband is extremely heat-sensitive, test your brick material first, allowing it to set up and checking its temperature periodically as it dries, to determine whether it is safe for your purposes.

When your mold is ready, pour in plaster or cement until it is about one-third full. Allow the material to harden and then place the contraband on top. Now add enough material to fill the mold, let it harden, and voila!

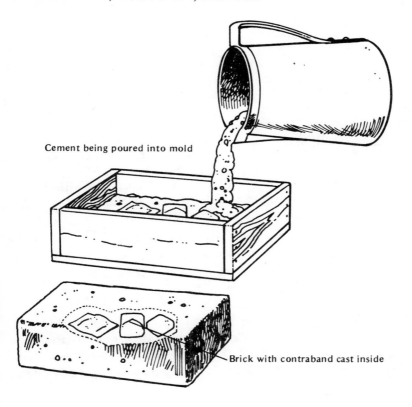

Cement being poured into mold

Brick with contraband cast inside

I have never seen border officials empty a builder's truck and smash its contents to pieces, so I assume this method is pretty safe.

A similar technique can be applied to suit different situations. Paving slabs, fancy tiles, or smaller items like ashtrays, drinking mugs, and teapots could all be used. Keep in mind, though, that the small articles would have to be made of plaster or clay, both very breakable materials. A cement teapot, if picked up by an official, might cause suspicion, and perhaps a hernia as well, which would doubtless prejudice him against you.

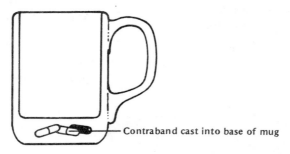

Contraband cast into base of mug

When using the tradesman cover, the good old wheelbarrow is well suited for stashing certain goods. The type of barrow with a tubular handlebar construction is best, as the handlebars will conceal quite large amounts of contraband. Insert the items into the bars and fill the end, using mud, clay, or plastic filler colored with sand or other camouflage. Once again, make sure the barrow is made to look well used. The inflatable type of barrow tire can also be adapted by deflating the inner tube, taping items between tire and tube, and inflating the tube again.

I am reminded at this point of an anecdote which says a great deal about smuggling techniques and the attitude of many customs officials and security officers. At a large factory in central Colorado, there once worked a guy who had certainly "got the measure" of the factory security man.

Every night after work, this guy could be seen pushing a wheelbarrow out of the factory and past the gatehouse. Every night the security man would stop him and search the barrow, but it was always empty. This went on for over a year. Many people were stopped by the security man and quite a few were found to be smuggling goods out of the factory, but always the barrow was empty. Eventually the time came for the security man to leave, and on his last night he stopped the guy with the barrow and said, "Look, I finish here tonight, so it really doesn't matter any more, but I must know, are you lifting anything?"

The man looked calmly back at the security guard and replied, "Yes—wheelbarrows!"

Contraband hidden in tubular handlebars

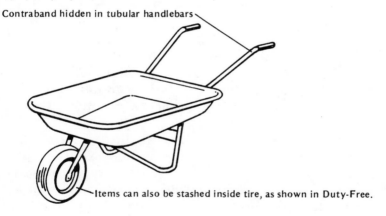

Items can also be stashed inside tire, as shown in Duty-Free.

Riding a pedal cycle or small moped through a checkpoint is a variation on the above theme. Use the framework of the machine to secrete the items, and make sure that any saddle bags or baskets are well filled with perfectly normal, everyday items.

Access to the inside of most tubular framed machines can be gained by removing the front fork assembly, the pedal-footrest assembly, and so on. If difficulty is experienced in obtaining access, most of the tubular sections can be opened by heating the sealed end and prying out the turned-in or bent-over edges.

The bicycle pump itself can also be used. Remove the piston assembly from inside the unit and shorten it as shown below in order to create the required space without completely disabling the pump.

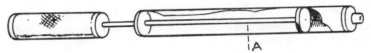

Shorten the piston rod (A) so that the pump will hold contraband but still close fully.

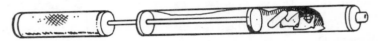

Another useful cover is that of the student or professor. The typewriter, a tool of the academic trade, is an innocuous piece of equipment. Its possession requires little justification in the eyes of most customs and border authorities; yet if it is doctored in the following manner, it can provide a very useful amount of space.

As designs vary considerably, it is best to refer to the handbook for specific disassembly instructions. If you have no handbook, obtain a cheap model to experiment with. Even a broken one will do. The idea is to remove the carriage assembly from the machine and then the roller from the carriage. Sometimes it will be possible to remove the end pieces of the roller to gain access to the inside. If this is not the case, however, simply hacksaw off one of the end pieces as shown on the next page.

Contraband may be inserted quite easily into the hollow roller. The end piece is refitted, using a powerful adhesive like Super Glue. Sometimes the rubber covering on the roller causes problems when this method is used, so if you find that the machine you intend to use requires hacksaw treatment, peel back the rubber layer before commencing. A sharp knife slid under the rubber and worked around the roller will usually do the trick. You can also stand the roller in hot water for ten minutes or so beforehand as this helps to soften the rubber.

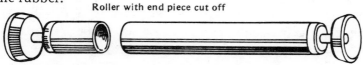

Roller with end piece cut off

If difficulty is encountered replacing end piece, use a short piece of tube of a diameter slightly smaller than that of roller to support both sections.

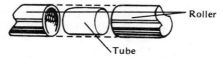

Roller

Tube

The toilet roll method can also be used on the typewriter ribbon.

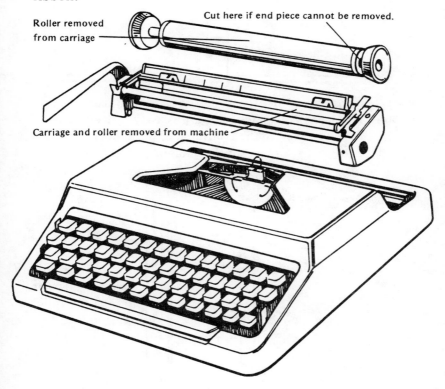

Roller removed from carriage

Cut here if end piece cannot be removed.

Carriage and roller removed from machine

The looseleaf notebook can also be part of the student or professor cover. The type of notebook that is most easily converted consists of a front and back cover, in between which is a fixed plastic spine with three or four ring fasteners to which papers are attached. These folders are readily available from most stationery or office supply outlets, and can be adapted as shown below.

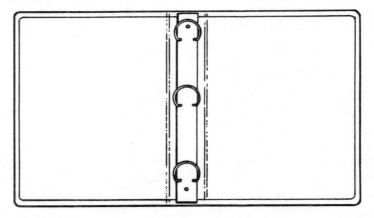

Remove the spine from the covers and, using a sharp hobby knife or razor blade, cut out a cavity or trough of sufficient depth to receive the contraband. Once the contraband is in place, refit using Super Glue or a similar adhesive.

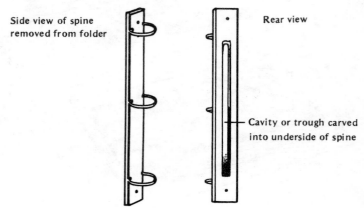

Side view of spine
removed from folder

Rear view

Cavity or trough carved
into underside of spine

Replace the spine between the covers and insert several pages in the notebook to complete the disguise. Some of these folders have the spine riveted onto the cover, and in these cases it will be necessary to drill them out to remove the spine. When reassembling, always use rivets, even if originally the spine was secured only with adhesive.

An old but useful stash, eminently suited to the student, professor, or collector cover, is the hollow book. Select a large, hardbound volume. Open the book roughly a quarter of the way through, and insert a marker. Then turn the book over and repeat the process on the other side. You will end up with the center half of the book isolated. It is this central section of pages that will be adapted.

With a very sharp blade, cut a cavity the size and shape required. Do not be greedy and try to fit too much into one book. It is far better to use several doctored books which are mixed in with unaltered ones. Make sure that the contraband is secure, and will not fall out if the book is lifted and shaken. Very often, an examiner will lift and shake a book without bothering to look closely inside it. The extra security here is the fact that the first quarter of the pages are un-

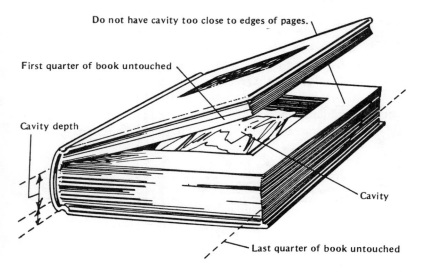

Do not have cavity too close to edges of pages.

First quarter of book untouched

Cavity depth

Cavity

Last quarter of book untouched

touched, and if the cavity is located as shown above, even
casually flipping through the book will not reveal the stash.
Don't overdo the weight of the items, and always have a
plausible reason for possessing the book. Make sure you
know something about the author to make your cover believ-
able.

Students, professors, and almost everyone else carry pens
of one kind or another, and many can be swiftly turned into
useful stashes. The best kind to use are felt tips, the smart
looking pens, not the fat markers which appear fairly suspicious if carried on the person in any quantity. The markers,
however, could easily be adapted as shown and repacked in
the original box. They are obtainable in sets, and it is quite
conceivable that such a set would be purchased as a gift!
The thinner type of felt tip pen can be carried two or three at
a time in a jacket pocket without attracting any attention.
Always carry this kind as you would carry a normal pen, in
your top pocket or another likely place. Make no attempt to
hide it.

Although not intended to be refilled, such a pen will have
a removable top piece that allows access to the internal ink-
ing tube, an ink-soaked felt cylinder. With a few taps on a
hard surface it should drop out. If it doesn't, simply insert
any thin object and lever it out. The bottom nib remains
fixed. Insert the items—I have found it possible to fit six
rounds of .22 or a couple of rounds of .38 into a slender felt-
tip pen. Obviously, there are many permutations. From the
removed ink tube, cut enough of a slice to fit over the top of
the contraband, giving the impression, in the remote chance
of the cap being removed, that the pen is untouched.

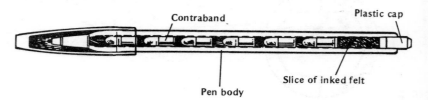

Contraband   Plastic cap

Pen body   Slice of inked felt

The nib of such pens retains enough ink after the guts are removed to write a full page, so if tested, the pen will stand up nicely. When replacing the plastic cap, apply a small amount of glue as extra security.

While the tradesman, student, professor, and collector covers are effective, you might feel more comfortable with a sporty image. Many people, whether on vacation or going to work, take along a ball of some kind for a quick game during lunch break or whatever, and depending on the size and design of the ball, quite large quantities of contraband can be carried using the methods below.

If the ball is of the sewn leather type, it will probably be made of a number of sections or patches. Using a sharp knife, cut along the sides of one of the patches and open it like a flap or door. With some balls it may also be necessary to burst an internal bladder. (Internal bladders can easily be repaired with a bicycle puncture repair kit.) Insert the items and secure them in place using duct tape or another powerful adhesive tape. To reseal, use an awl to sew the flap back in place and apply a thin layer of clear rubber cement as a safety measure.

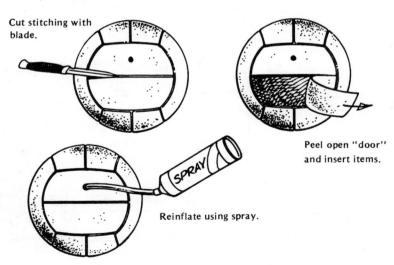

Cut stitching with blade.

Peel open "door" and insert items.

Reinflate using spray.

The ball is reinflated with a latex-based aerosol substance used for sealing and reinflating burst tires on vehicles. Brand names may vary, but the product should be available from auto accessory outlets and garages.

Treat the ball so that it looks well used, scuffed and battered. Take care not to overdo the weight of the contraband and make sure that it is protected from the aerosol. Remember, it is necessary only to make the ball look genuine—it need not hold the correct pressure.

Baseball bats, tennis rackets, and other sports equipment of this type can be adapted to carry contraband the same way tool handles are modified. With most aluminum alloy equipment it is possible to insert items without extensive drilling or cutting.

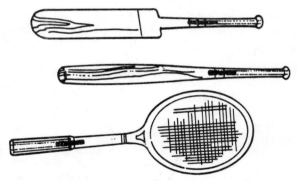

Contraband shown hidden in handles

The inflatable air mattresses or rafts that many people take on vacation are also readily adapted to conceal contraband. Items like small caliber ammunition can be pushed into the mattress through the inlet valve. Actually, the word *valve* used in this context is an exaggeration. The kind of mattress to which I'm referring generally only sports holes and is inflated by mouth or, at best, a primitive pump.

For larger items, split the seam on one of the sections and insert goods. Reseal using a plastic adhesive. Few people deflate an air mattress completely after use, and the odd piece of contraband will pass unnoticed during a search. Once again I emphasize the point: Don't overdo it. We're talking *air* mattresses here, get it?

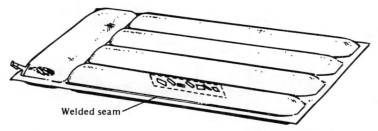

Welded seam

Nothing could be more commonplace and inconspicuous than food, and bags of groceries, lunch boxes, and picnics lend themselves to conversion most readily.

Apart from such obvious hides as cornflake boxes and bags of sugar or flour, a loaf of bread will conceal faily large items with a high degree of security.

For sliced bread, carefully remove and retain the wrapping; then remove about a quarter of the slices from the loaf, and cut out a cavity from the remaining bread as shown in the diagram below. Once the contraband is in place, replace the rest of the slices and rewrap the loaf securely.

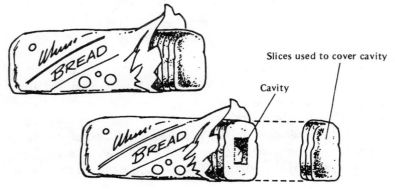

Slices used to cover cavity

Cavity

For unsliced loaves, the easiest method is to carefully cut slices of the crust away from the outside of the loaf, gently push the items to be hidden inside, and fix the pieces of crust back in place with any suitable adhesive. The loaf can be packed out with lumps of bread pulled from another loaf if necessary.

Pieces of crust removed and contraband pushed into loaf

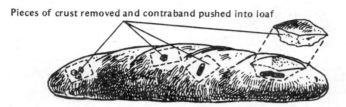

A variation on the canned food method shown in *Duty-Free* is detailed below. It is not necessary to remove the label from the can in this method. Remove the lid from the can using a butterfly opener or similar opener that leaves no material from the lid attached to the can mouth. Empty the contents into a bowl and stash the items to be hidden in the can.

Next, obtain a lid from a can of a slightly greater diameter than the hide can. Grind or file the lid until it fits snugly into the mouth of the hide can and does not look out of place. To prevent the lid from becoming overheated and discolored during the shaping process, always cool it off in water after a few seconds of grinding. The correct way in which to file the lid in order to maintain a circular shape is shown on the next page.

Once you are happy with the fit of the lid, apply a thin shelf of epoxy resin to the inside mouth of the tin and allow it to harden. This shelf will support the new lid. Add a small amount of genuine contents to the can—beans, carrots, or whatever is indicated on the label. This will help if the can is partially opened during a search. Apply a bead of adhesive to the underside of the outside edge of the lid and place it in the

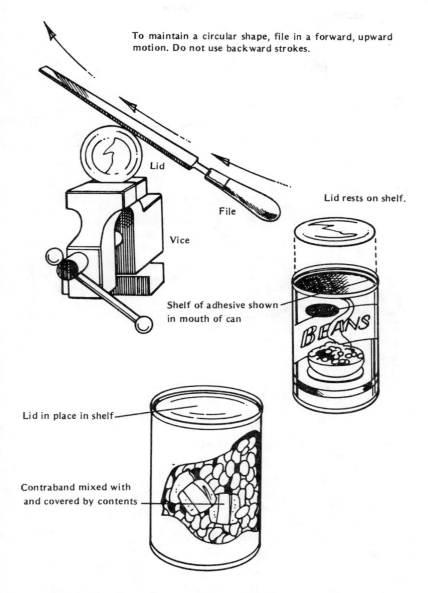

To maintain a circular shape, file in a forward, upward motion. Do not use backward strokes.

Lid

File

Vice

Lid rests on shelf.

Shelf of adhesive shown in mouth of can

BEANS

Lid in place in shelf

Contraband mixed with and covered by contents

mouth of the can, resting on the epoxy shelf. If the lid requires jiggling around, use a strong magnet or suction cup.

Vehicle and persons entering "secure area" with contraband hidden in:
1. Special bricks and other items
2. Ladders
3. Tool handles
4. Lunchbox containing bread and other food
5. Ball for kicking during lunch hour, breaks, and so on

Household items, seemingly innocent, can often be made to do double duty.

Although I dislike mentioning specific contraband (not for any moral reason, but rather because it tends to condition the reader into thinking that the hide is suitable for only that specific article), I cannot resist detailing the following treatment for cardboard boxes, which can be used whenever the need to covertly transport explosives arises.

First of all, obtain a length of "det cord," the fast, almost instantaneously burning cord used to detonate explosive devices in demolition and quarry work. It should not be confused with slow-burning time fuse. Research indicates that the main ingredient in det cord is P.E.T.N., and it is often sold under the brand name Instacord or Primacord.

Use a sharp blade to cut open the det cord, and remove the center filling of P.E.T.N. (or equivalent).

Next, obtain some acetone. This is a clear, smelly liquid used as a powerful solvent, and is usually obtainable from hardware stores, dry cleaning equipment suppliers, or garages. Half-fill a suitable glass container with the acetone, and put it into a pan of preheated water to gently heat the acetone. NEVER try to heat the acetone directly over a heat source, and NEVER heat the pan of water while the acetone container is in place.

Next (while the acetone container is still in the hot water, *but making sure that the pan holding the hot water is well clear of the heat source!*), add a small amount of the P.E.T.N. to the acetone, stirring constantly with a *glass* or heat resistant *plastic* implement. Do NOT use a metal spoon! As the P.E.T.N. dissolves, continue adding small amounts until a stage is reached when, even after prolonged continual stirring, the P.E.T.N. will not dissolve further.

At this point, add a small amount of mineral oil and pour the whole solution into a container suitable to the size and shape of the cardboard or paper to be doctored.

The box, or whatever, is left to soak in the solution for about half an hour, then removed and put aside to *air dry*. Do NOT place on fireplace or in an oven! When the cardboard or paper is dry, it will be a powerful high explosive that can be taken anywhere without attracting attention, and it will survive close examination by officials. The explosive can be detonated in a normal manner by using a detonator (blasting cap).

I would recommend using cardboard packing cases for this method, as it will be the objects contained therein, not the box, that will be subjected to scrutiny. Small pieces of the cardboard can always be torn off for use in an emergency! Most papers can be used, however, as long as they are not the glossy, shiny type.

The quantities involved are determined by the amount of explosive required, but generally speaking use two thirds by weight of acetone mixed with one third by weight of P.E.T.N. The amount of mineral oil to be added is roughly two percent of the volume of the solution.

The oil has the effect of reducing the visual indications of explosive in the cardboard or paper. It may be better to experiment with different quantities before making the final mix.

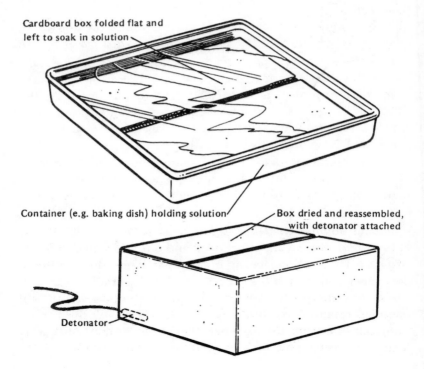

Cardboard box folded flat and left to soak in solution

Container (e.g. baking dish) holding solution

Box dried and reassembled, with detonator attached

Detonator

Another innocent-looking household item that can be easily adapted is the toilet roll or kitchen paper towel roll. Carefully unroll the paper for about half of its length and, using a sharp knife or blade, cut out a cavity from the remaining paper as shown in the diagram. Insert item to be concealed and rewind the roll. Make sure that the cavity is centrally placed so that it cannot be seen from the edge of the roll. Always replace original packaging.

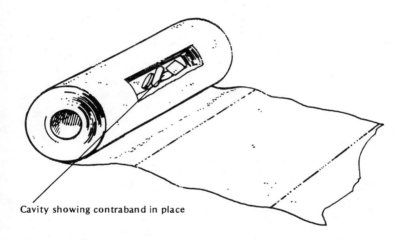

Cavity showing contraband in place

For added security, never use this method to convey very heavy items, as undue weight is usually the only reason that the article would attract attention. Under normal circumstances, few officials will unroll 100 feet of toilet paper!

Keys abound in our lives today, and many of them, if adapted in the following manner, can provide useful little stashes. The simplest key to use is the large, long padlock key shown on the next page.

With a sharp hacksaw, cut off a slice from the end of the key and retain. Next, using a fine bit on a hobby drill, bore out a cavity from the inside of the key as shown. Refit the end piece using glue, or a thin film of plastic car body-filler.

File to a neat finish, and attach to a key chain (on which you could have several more of the same!).

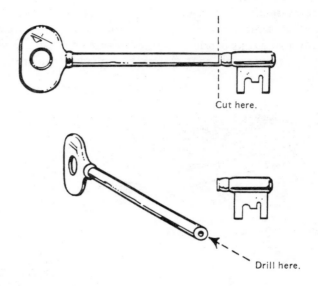

Cut here.

Drill here.

The next best type of key to use is similar to the first except that it is of the hollow type useful for substances. A false end is attached, made from car body-filler or metal putty and molded into the correct shape. Or an end stop or plug is inserted over the powder or whatever, and pushed well home. Imagine you are filling an old muzzle loader to get the picture.

At first glance, it would seem that the effort involved is not justified, due to the small amount of space. However, if you have a bunch of say, five keys on the car ignition key ring, and colleagues have a similar quantity . . . Do you know how much coke makes an ounce?

An alternative to the cigarette method shown in *Duty-Free* is given next, but I strongly recommend that you only use the technique as follows. Always ensure that the adapted packs of cigarettes are carried among other, similar packs that have not been altered. Either invest in a commercial machine for rewrapping the packs in cellophane, or practice doing the same manually. Any excise seals that should be on the packs must be replaced carefully, and make sure that the total number of packs carried through does not exceed the limit.

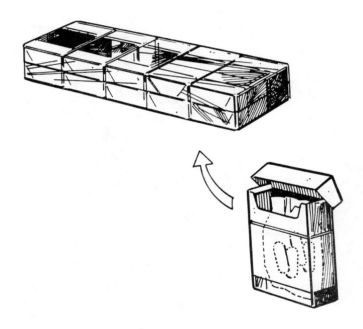

Once you have selected the packs of cigarettes to be adapted (obviously the king size type are best suited), remove the cigarettes from the pack and with a sharp blade slice off the filter tips. Glue the severed filters together as shown below so that they are in the same position as they would be if in the pack. Place the contraband in the box, and cover with some kind of stop plate so that when the filter tips are replaced on top they will sit neatly as in an unaltered pack. Used correctly, this is an excellent stash.

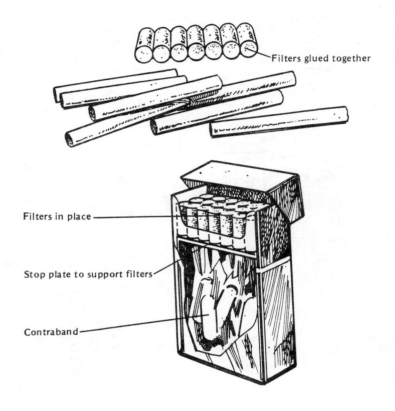

Cameras make good hides, as unless the country or area to be left or entered prohibits cameras, they are generally looked on with a degree of respect. This is especially true when you mention or imply that the film contains "some lovely shots of your beautiful country." Cameras can be very confusing to the uninitiated, and the fear of exposing or damaging the film, thereby effectively ruining a holiday or business trip and "giving a bad impression of the country," usually deters close examination by the guard or official.

Furthermore, the guard or official (unless you are unlucky enough to come across a camera buff) will not want to show his ignorance of the workings of the camera by fumbling around with it in a foolish manner.

A useful ploy is to ask if it would be all right to take a picture of the guard himself for your album. Pandering to the official's ego is generally very effective.

Rolls of exposed film in cans can also be utilized as shown below.

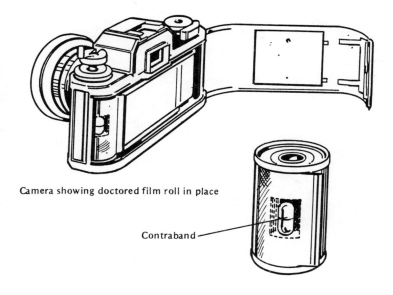

Camera showing doctored film roll in place

Contraband

Use the toilet roll method to form a cavity in film roll and place in can or camera.

A smoker's pipe can also be used to convey small items or substances using the technique shown below. Always make sure that the bowl of the pipe has some old tobacco in it. A dirty, tar-stained mouthpiece may prevent close examination. Leave the pipe lying in a conspicuous place, such as on the dashboard of a vehicle or protruding from a jacket pocket.

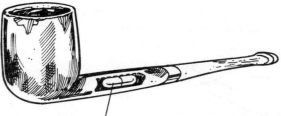

Contraband hidden in stem of pipe. Use a drill to enlarge its diameter if necessary.

Plants or flowers well established in a pot are a well-used way of transporting items through security checks. Nevertheless, under the correct circumstances, this method is still very effective.

Contraband hidden in earth

The kind of large wooden coathanger that has a separate roller underneath for trousers may also be used to conceal contraband. The roller will come apart in an obvious fashion, and may be used as ready storage space, or you can drill or bore out the shoulders of the hanger, insert items, and refill with car body-filler.

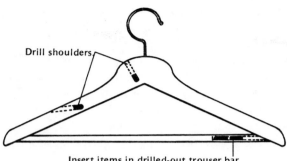

Drill shoulders

Insert items in drilled-out trouser bar.

Another method of smuggling quantities of very valuable substances involves the doctoring of record albums. Allowing for minor production differences, the width of the average album at its center is one-eighth to one-tenth of an inch. By the *center* I refer to the slightly raised middle area of the disk, not the hole! Attempts to conceal items in the hole will create problems for even the most ingenious among you, so forget it! Seriously though, by using the following method it will be possible to move a whole range of substances covertly and safely right under the noses of prying officials (at least until they read this it will be).

The first stage is to select the thickest disk you can find—as I said there are variations—and to remove the circular title label by steaming or carefully applying an adhesive solvent to the label. Take care when steaming also, as excessive exposure to the steam will warp the record severely.

Once the label is removed place it to one side and allow to dry. This label will be the camouflage for the finished product, so don't damage it. Next obtain some sort of small, flat-ended tool or a nonserrated edged knife, or .025" feeler gauge and, after heating the edge of the tool for a few seconds with a lighter, begin to scrape away the surface of the central, raised portion. Take care doing this as too much pressure will simply push the tool bit straight through the disk, ruining the job.

Done carefully, only a thin layer of the record's surface is left on the opposite side, which appears perfectly normal when examined. By scraping out several trenches, a considerable quantity of your chosen substance can be concealed.

The final stage is to level off the layers of substance and to replace the label. To ensure that the stash is both secure and undetectable, the label should be soaked in clear resin and allowed to harden before replacing. It can be affixed to the disk using a few tiny drops of glue. The completed item can be sent through the post or carried through a check with confidence. Were a whole boxful of similarly treated albums sent as part of an export order, then obviously much more substance could be moved in one go.

Another method of evading duty or even making a tidy little profit relies on the fact that most national customs regulations allow a greater quantity of wine than spirits to be brought back from a trip abroad. Regulations usually allow two to three liters of wine and one liter of spirit before duty is payable, spirits obviously commanding a much higher price and producing more tax in the home country. The difference in price of spirits bought in some countries between those of their homebought counterparts is often tremendous. This is especially applicable to top-of-the-market spirits like twelve-year-old malt whiskey.

Quite simply, all one has to do to avoid paying duty on such spirits is to decant them into wine bottles, making sure, of course, that the label, cork, and foil seal appear genuine. You must also fool officials making a cursory check. This is achieved by selecting green bottles which make the liquor indistinguishable from wine.

Always keen to encourage free enterprise, several outlets in popular tourist countries even supply a do-it-yourself kit which includes the genuine foil seals and corks, all for a very reasonable price.

My own favorite spot for spirit purchases is a small republic in Italy about ten miles from the Adriatic coast, called San

Marino. This place seems not to believe in taxation of any kind, and the prices of a whole range of goods are fantastic. It makes a great port of call for any vacation. If you ever get there, look up a place called Lucy's Off Sales and have a few words with a guy called Dino. He'll be only too pleased to show you the ropes regarding the "wine fiddle."

A face sponge can be cut into two sections, a cavity cut into the lower section, and items inserted. It is not necessary to cut out a proper cavity as used with more solid objects, but merely remove the top half inch or so of sponge. Do the same to the bottom face of the top section, and it will be found that even with quite large items inserted the two sections will join together perfectly with no signs of tampering. Fix the two sections back in place using a suitable adhesive, according to what material the sponge is made from. Doctor the sponge to give an impression of wear and tear. Have the sponge slightly wet, as this will explain any increase in weight if the sponge is examined. Bits of pubic hair, dirt, and old soap on the sponge will deter close examination.

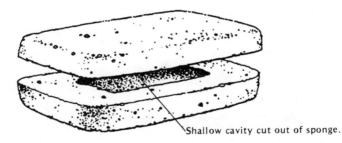

Shallow cavity cut out of sponge.

Use in conjunction with doctored soap and other toiletries from Duty Free.

A useful twist on normal practice that I have employed with great success makes use of the packaging around an item rather than the item itself. I'm speaking of the fairly elaborate polystyrene packing that manufacturers seem to have in excess and use at the slightest excuse to effectively bury the item in question. Favorite products for this treatment are

electronic and electrical units like radios and home computers. Those of you familiar with the home computer craze
will know exactly what I mean. The average program (on cassette) for these machines measures two by three inches, and
comes in a polystyrene box measuring about two square feet.

Anyway, choose a unit that has a considerable amount of
packing and carefully remove it. Use a blade or a hot knife
and cut a slice from the packaging as shown below. Cut out a
cavity of sufficient size for your requirements and insert the
contraband. Replace the slice, and secure using polystyrene
cement. Be careful with the adhesive you use, as certain glues
will melt the polystyrene. If necessary, touch up the area that
has been doctored with paint or apply extra packing tape to
disguise the work.

This method is very effective, as the tendency among customs officers is to unpack items, examine them to determine
their value and to check for hidden contraband and, if you're
lucky, give you back the item (after a half-hearted attempt
to repack it), then move on to the next victim. The packing is
usually overlooked, and hardly ever torn to pieces to check
for cavities!

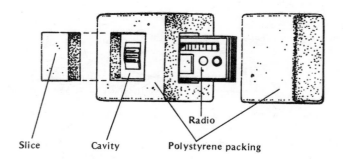

Slice   Cavity   Radio   Polystyrene packing

An excellent place of concealment that I have never
known to fail (this doesn't mean it *can't* fail) is inside the
capacitor, an electronic component common to 90 percent
of all electronic equipment. These can take many forms, but

it is the larger diameter can type that is most suited for our purposes.

Select a radio, television or other piece of equipment with a large capacitor in the circuit. The diagrams below show a few examples of capacitors and chokes, which are of a similar construction, and also their respective circuit diagram symbols so that you may ascertain whether the equipment contains capacitors or chokes before you start disassembling the unit.

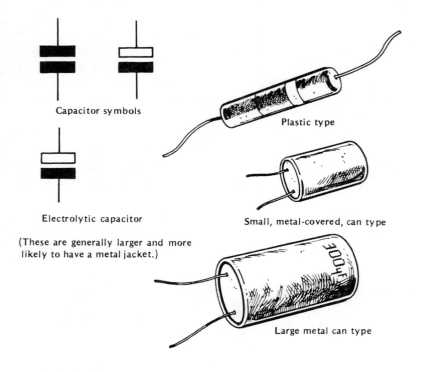

Capacitor symbols

Plastic type

Electrolytic capacitor

Small, metal-covered, can type

(These are generally larger and more likely to have a metal jacket.)

Large metal can type

The smaller capacitor cans are usually made from ceramic or plastic, and may be drilled to create a cavity for storage purposes. However, some of the small ones and almost all the larger cans will be contained in a metal case similar in appearance to a large flashlight battery. The lip on the mouth of the case can be carefully levered open and the cover plate removed. Once the cap is removed, simply drill out the internal substance, insert the desired items, and reseal. Fasten the cap in place with adhesive, and solder the component back into its original position in the equipment. Some smoothing capacitors used in TVs, power converter (D.C. from A.C.) units and so on, are huge, and if you are in the export business proper the possibilities using this method are countless.

Another plus for this method is that in certain circumstances, depending on the nature of the equipment involved, the doctored can will *not* prevent the unit from working! Admittedly, it will not work well, but should the customs authority decide to plug in and switch on (very unlikely anyway), the unit will operate. Combined with the fact that no visible signs of tampering remain, this makes the capacitator can one of the safest methods of conveying items or substances around.

On some cans it may not be possible to lever open the lip due to their design. If this is the case, simply cut off the end section and, when the items are stashed, refit and secure with powerful adhesive. Also, the contents of some cans resemble a mishmash mixture of damp paper and bits of metal. This can be safely scooped out, or items pushed in around it.

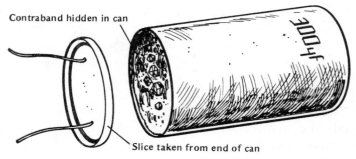

Contraband hidden in can

Slice taken from end of can

These cans are generally made from soft aluminum, and can be cut with a hacksaw, or even a steak knife.

If you intend to use the can hide, why not have a look inside your selected piece of equipment to see if it contains a transformer of some sort? Transformers are commonly found in electronic hardware in a variety of sizes, some of which are very useful indeed. With minor differences only, the usual type of transformer looks like the illustration below, and is doctored in the following manner.

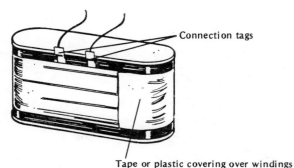

Connection tags

Tape or plastic covering over windings

First cut through the wires that connect the internal windings of the transformer to the external connection point or points. Retain the tabs. The windings themselves will be covered with either tape or a plastic coating. In either case, remove the covering to gain access to the wire. The next stage is to simply unwind the transformer windings until you are left with only a central core which will be nothing more than a frame on which the wire has been wound. It will not be necessary to remove all the wire, but merely enough to accommodate the contraband. Fix the item in place with tape and begin the fun task of rewinding enough of the wire to disguise the contraband. Do this in such a way so as to enable the transformer to be casually examined without it attracting attention, replacing external connections and so on. Refit the unit into the radio, power supply or whatever, and away you go.

Michael Connor

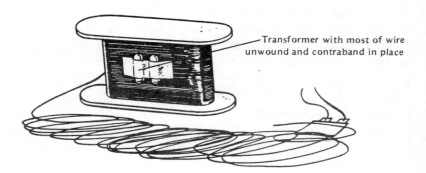

Transformer with most of wire unwound and contraband in place

A little-used technique (for obvious reasons) is to feed an item, suitably wrapped, to a large dog. Either force feed the

Dog runs through gate alone. If there is a crowd or the weather is bad, the animal will often pass unnoticed.

item to the animal, or conceal it in an appetizing piece of meat. Where local regulations permit, take the animal across the border as your pet. Otherwise send it through on its own and lure it back into your control on the other side.

It may be necessary to destroy the animal in order to reclaim the item. If the object is wrapped in a well-rounded piece of nondigestable, nonpoisonous material such as polythene, however, there is a likelihood of nature returning the object to you in due course. Depending on the size of the object (and the dog) it may also be possible to make the animal regurgitate the package by inducing vomiting. If you intend to use this method, do so as near to the crossing time as possible, so as to reduce the chance of the animal showing signs of distress and attracting unwanted attention.

Many other types of small electric components can be adapted to conceal contraband, but a very nice technique that few people have heard about and which is extremely difficult to detect is as follows. First of all, obtain a selection of components from a typical domestic unit such as a radio or cassette player. Next, select items of suitably sized contraband, and after first sealing them in a protective wrapping, dip them into a thick plaster solution, modeling clay, plastic car body-filler, or any other substance that will harden gradually and can be molded into shape.

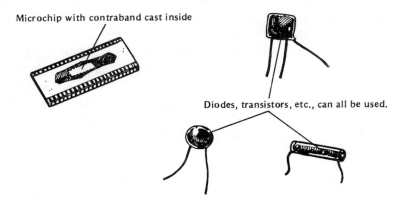

Microchip with contraband cast inside

Diodes, transistors, etc., can all be used.

Before the material hardens completely, mold the blob containing the contraband into a shape resembling that of any of the electronic components, attach legs, pins, and so on to the item, and leave to set. (The legs and pins can be cut beforehand from genuine components.) When dry, paint or color the fake components in a suitable manner, and resolder into a position inside the selected unit or units.

Exact reproduction of the shape and size of the components is not absolutely necessary, as very few customs officials and border guards will have access to circuit diagrams of the equipment for reference purposes, and even if the unit is stripped down, no visible signs of tampering will exist. Microchips are easily faked, and some pieces of electronic equipment contain literally dozens of them.

A great number of home and business computers now on the market, especially in the Atari line, offer programs to accompany the hardware in the form of ROMs. For those not computer oriented, ROM means Read Only Memory. It is an information chip that is not user accessible, to the extent that the user cannot alter the information contained in it. Examples of the more common ROMs are the game cartridges that plug into the top of the computer. These ROMs take the form of more or less square, plastic boxes, from the base of which protrudes the section of circuit board that connects the cartridge to the computer; a plug type of affair.

All the ROMs that I have adapted have been sealed with a single, centrally placed screw. The screw is usually concealed beneath the program name sticker, and great care must be taken to remove this sticker without leaving telltale signs of tampering. Use steam or glue solvent applied sparingly and worked under the sticker, peeling off a few inches at a time. By running your fingernail over the surface of the sticker, it will be possible to determine the side that holds the screw head, thereby saving the unnecessary removal of both sides of the sticker.

Once the sticker is removed, unscrew the two halves of the box and insert the items in the space available. This will vary according to the number of chips in the ROM. Reseal the two halves carefully, and always replace in the original packaging.

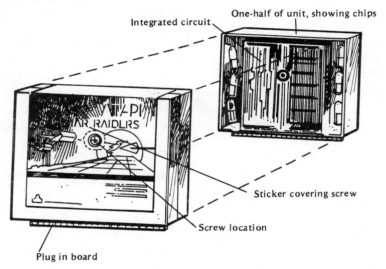

Integrated circuit

One-half of unit, showing chips

Sticker covering screw

Screw location

Plug in board

The fluorescent tube lights used in mobile home vehicles make useful hides. Choose only the white or colored type, and adapt them in the following manner.

Obtain a stout box, and make a hole in one side of it the diameter of the light to be doctored. Insert the tube into the box through the hole until all but one end connector is covered. Using a small drill, make a hole in the center of the end connector. These lights contain a gas, and when punctured suddenly will explode (actually, I think they *implode,* but this isn't a physics lesson). If, however, the gas is released through the carefully drilled hole, there is no problem. Now you know what the box is for! Once the gas is released—this will happen with an audible hiss—gently heat the end connector with a cigarette lighter, working the end piece back and forth with grips or pliers at the same time. Eventually the end piece will become loose enough to twist off without damaging the glass tube. Simply insert items; again, do not overdo it. It is unlikely that the lights will be disturbed during an inspection, but just in case they are, you don't want them to weigh nine pounds each, do you? Replace the end piece with strong adhesive. Replace doctored tubes in holders or store as spares. Some of the smaller lights used in mobile homes are not fluorescent, but contain a filament. Apart from breaking this during end piece removal, and not having to drill the gas escape hole, the operation is the same!

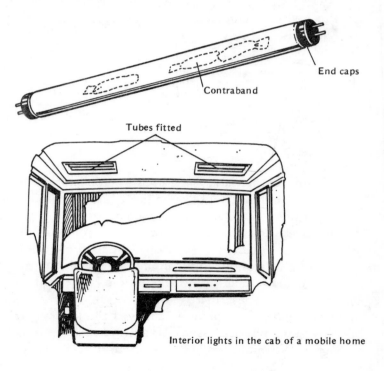

End caps

Contraband

Tubes fitted

Interior lights in the cab of a mobile home

While we are in your mobile home, so to speak, take a look at the table tops. If they are of formica-covered chipboard construction, the following method can be used with excellent results.

Remove the outer edge covering as shown in the diagram, and retain. If no such covering is fitted, but the table is of a fairly thick construction, measure up and make one to use as a covering yourself. Using a suitable tool, depending upon the type of wood from which the table is constructed, carve out a cavity of the dimensions you require. Insert items and re-attach the outer edge cover. Use both adhesive and staples or screws. Alternatively, it may be possible to remove the top layer of formica and carve out a cavity from above. If you do this, always fit a false top in between the formica covering and the cavity. Secure well and disguise as carefully as possible.

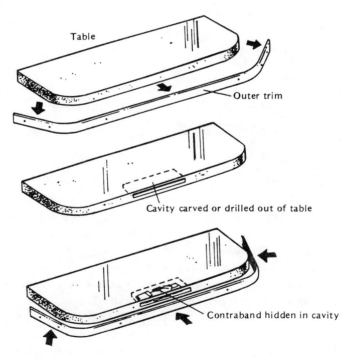

Table

Outer trim

Cavity carved or drilled out of table

Contraband hidden in cavity

If the mobile home does not sport impressive interior decoration, now is the time to give it a refit. Not only does a cluttered interior help to deter thorough examination, but numerous drawers, fold-out beds, cooker tops, and so on can provide countless hiding places.

Rarely used and very reliable stashes can be formed from the wooden poles that are often used to hang curtains. Remove any end cap, if fitted, and bore out a cavity as in the ladder technique. Always fit an internal plug over the cavity and secure with adhesive. Replace the end cap or, if not originally fitted, obtain one from an accessory shop. The thinner plastic rails used for curtains can also be drilled with a fine bit. In certain cases, the hems of the curtains themselves can be used to conceal contraband, both at the top and bottom, and also behind any backing material that may be fitted.

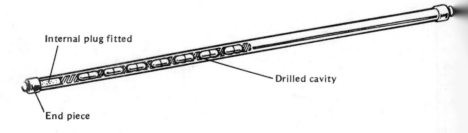

Internal plug fitted

Drilled cavity

End piece

The other most effective mobile home hides are inside the water tank if it is the underfloor type, or inside the toilet pan. Find a willing volunteer to insert the items, suitably wrapped, inside a thick, stinking piece of s————. Unless you are under suspicion anyway, no one will bother to search through the contents of a recently used head.

A cooking pot of some description is another item that can be found among campers, caravaners, or even the homeless refugees who roam certain areas of the globe. Find a pot large enough to carry your chosen contraband, and if new, generally abuse it to give the appearance of age and use. Melt a sufficient amount of cooking fat in the pan and insert the items, again suitably wrapped. Greaseproof paper and a layer of aluminum foil or an oven bag should do. Put it into the fat just before it hardens during cooling. Don't be greedy and wedge the entire bottom of the pan with contraband. Space a few items here and there. That way, even if the pot is dipped, the contraband is unlikely to be detected.

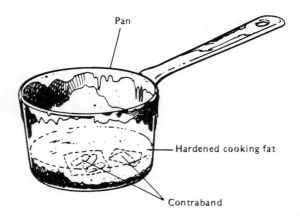

Pan

Hardened cooking fat

Contraband

There are a variety of button badge machines on the market now, and these can be easily used to construct innocent looking caches. The type of machine you obtain will depend, of course, on the cash you have available, but from experience I would say that they are so similar in operation that the following technique will apply to nearly all models.

Assemble the badge components according to manufacturer's instructions. With minor variations they will consist of a back piece with pin, a flat cover plate, the badge design itself, and a plastic cover or lens. When the handle on the machine is depressed, it crimps the flat cover plate around the edge of the backing piece, wrapping around the edge of the design and the plastic cover.

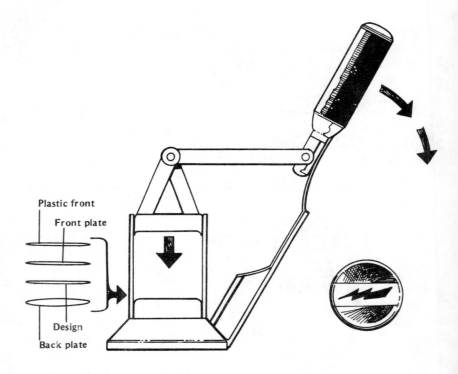

Plastic front
Front plate
Design
Back plate

Because the badge is round, and because the machine crimps the outer edge with some force, a small but useful space is created in the center of the front of the finished badge. This space is actually a thin pocket between the design and the cover plate, or between the cover plate and the backing piece, or both, depending on the machine design. Suitable contraband, in this case powders, microfilms, or one high-denomination bank note, could be used. (Other substances could no doubt be concealed; I have personally used the above items.) Extra pressure is required on the lever of the press, and in most cases, the badge is slightly deformed due to the hidden items. However, the deformation is not visible except under extremely close scrutiny, and a badge worn normally, say on a lapel, will pass untouched. Several people

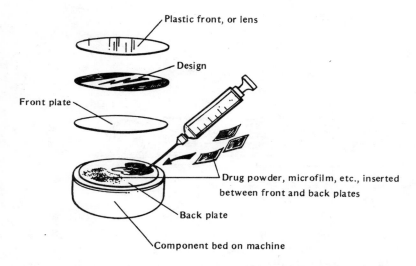

Plastic front, or lens

Design

Front plate

Drug powder, microfilm, etc., inserted
between front and back plates

Back plate

Component bed on machine

wearing badges can shift a fair bit of stuff! Where possible, obtain a design for the front of the badge that is calculated to appeal to the border staff: I love Pretoria, for example. This double bluff works well. Attention is deliberately drawn to the badge, thereby establishing a mental block on the part of the customs officer or guard as far as suspecting the badge is concerned. Designs may be simply cut from magazines.

Finally we come to vehicular hides. Although these usually require a fair amount of preparation, there is one spur of the moment method that I have seen used with great effect. It is, quite simply, to stash items inside heavy snow deposits on the roof of the vehicle! Use only the roof, as engine heat will melt snow from the hood, and the trunk will probably be opened during a search anyway. An official will rarely clear away the accumulated snow and ice from a vehicle's roof. Place the items to be moved on the roof a few hours to a day (depending on severity of conditions) before the crossing and drive carefully. If the items are wrapped in tin foil, the freezing conditions will soon secure them as effectively as any adhesive could do.

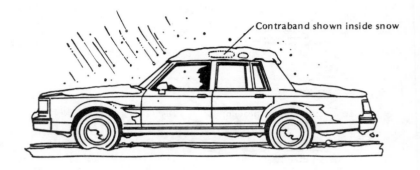

Contraband shown inside snow

Those of you with the good sense to have purchased a copy of *Duty-Free* will no doubt have noticed that there is an obvious improvement that can be simply made to the "beaten roof" method shown on pages 21 through 23. The improvement consists of fitting a suitably sized piece, or pieces, of hardboard or some similar material, between the internal headlining of the vehicle and the bottom of the beaten sections of roof. The hardboard effectively sandwiches the areas of beaten metal between itself and the outer,

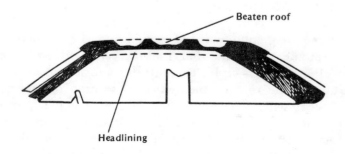

Beaten roof

Headlining

filled areas. If the headlining is poked or prodded during a search, a perfectly flat surface will be felt. With the headlining carefully replaced using Super Glue or a similar adhesive, the completed stash is undetectable.

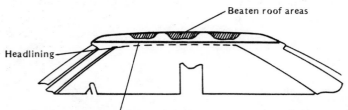

False roof fitted between headlining and inside bottom of beaten roof area

Another auto hide gaining popularity is inside the flexible stem of the vehicle seat belt anchor. The following method shows how to convert and disguise the stem for carrying contraband, but it should be noted that as soon as possible after the crossing the stem should be replaced with an unaltered one. There is an unwritten law that, if applied to this situation, would read: No sooner have you successfully crossed through customs with contraband concealed in the adapted stem of a flexible seat belt anchor than you will be involved in the only head-on wreck of your life!

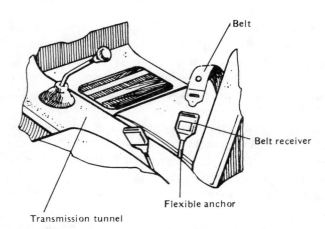

Unbolt the anchor stem from the floor and, having secured the unit in a vice, cut through the steel cable at a point three-quarters of the length from the base. Next cut

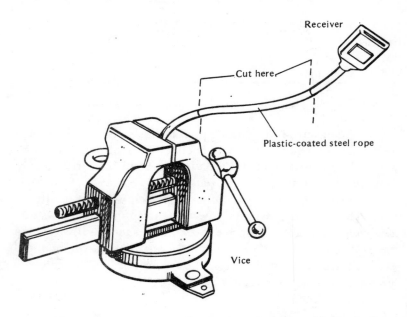

through the cable at a point farther down, sufficiently long to conceal the contraband, taking care not to exceed the support point. This support point is the distance up from the base that must be left intact in order to provide adequate support for the adapted stem (established by trial and error).

Discard the center piece of the steel cable that has been cut out. Now obtain a suitably colored piece of tube or pipe, of sufficient length to run from the base to the belt holder, and of an internal diameter to fit snugly over the bottom support piece and the remaining top piece incorporating the belt holder. Strip the covering from the two sections as shown below.

The pipe or tube must be strong enough to resist easy bending, but if the contraband to be moved is rigid—ammuni-

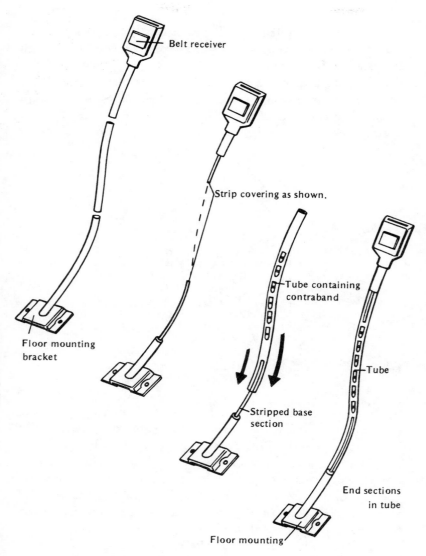

Belt receiver

Strip covering as shown.

Tube containing
contraband

Floor mounting
bracket

Tube

Stripped base
section

End sections
in tube

Floor mounting

tion, for example—this is not critical. The pipe is pushed home over the base piece which is secured in place on the floor. Next the contraband is inserted into the pipe, and finally the belt holder is pushed into the top end of the pipe.

A superb vehicular hide for relatively small items or substances within small containers or wrapping is inside the flexible brake hoses (flexi-hoses). These are the lengths of hydraulic pipe that carry brake fluid to the front wheels of a vehicle. As designs vary, it is best to refer to the vehicle handbook for specific disassembly instructions, but it is usually a simple process to remove the two front hoses.

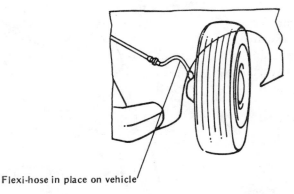

Flexi-hose in place on vehicle

Next obtain two lengths of hose of dimensions suitable to the contraband to be moved. Take care not to overdo the diameter or length of the hose. Remember that the hoses will not function after they have been doctored. Therefore it is not necessary to use genuine hose; any suitably shaped and colored piping may be employed. The only requirement is that the threaded connectors at each end of the length of hose are of the correct dimensions to engage with the connections on the wheel cylinders. The easiest way to achieve this is to remove the original connectors from the genuine brake hoses and affix them to the dummy hoses. Remember to insert items before finally fixing both end connectors in place on the hose.

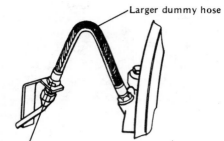

Larger dummy hose

This side of hose plugged

The next stage is to plug one end of the dummy pipe with plastic car body-filler. The idea is to prevent brake fluid entering the hose when the brake pedal is depressed. After the contraband is inserted, refit the hose in its correct position and away you go!

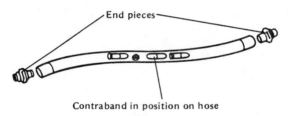

End pieces

Contraband in position on hose

Important: Obviously, this method will prevent the operation of the front brakes, and therefore care should be taken to brake early while driving and to spend some time getting used to the feel of the car before commencing the journey. It is surprising how quickly one does get used to driving with only the rear brakes, and the beauty of the method is that even a thorough examination of the vehicle will not reveal anything untoward.

The generator or alternator on a vehicle can also be easily adapted to conceal items. It makes no difference which is used, as they are both doctored in a similar fashion.

The purpose of the generator or alternator is to keep the battery well charged. Without the generator, the electrical demands of an average modern car would drain a fully charged battery in just over one hour, but this is of little consequence if the vehicle in question has only to pass through a short stretch of border. It is a simple matter to replace the generator completely, and it will only take fifteen minutes or so even under difficult circumstances.

As designs vary, it is best if you refer to the owner's manual for specific disassembly instructions. You will find, however, that it is possible with both generator and alternator to effectively remove the entire guts of the unit, leaving only a hollow shell. Obviously, for the sake of realism, it is necessary to replace the pulley wheel and some form of spindle for it to rotate on. Using the following methods, or variations thereon, it will be possible to achieve the desired effect, a generator that appears to be functional yet actually contains contraband.

Detach the wires from the rear of the generator (there will be two, one large and one small). Slacken the generator retaining and adjusting bolts, swing the unit towards the engine, and remove the fan belt. Remove the bolts, and the unit can now be lifted from the vehicle. At one end of the generator there will be two long retaining bolts. Remove

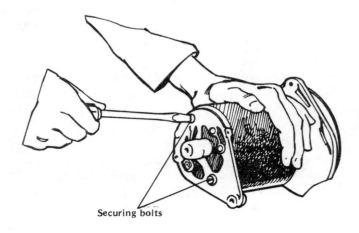

Securing bolts

them and lift off the end plate as shown in diagram below. The pulley assembly and the armature can now be withdrawn from the other end of the unit.

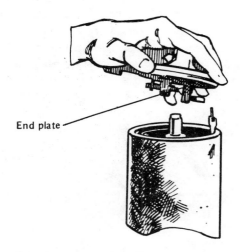

End plate

At this point refer to the workshop manual for armature disassembly instructions. Cut through the windings and center spindle at the point arrowed in diagram below. Insert

Cut through commutator assembly at this point.

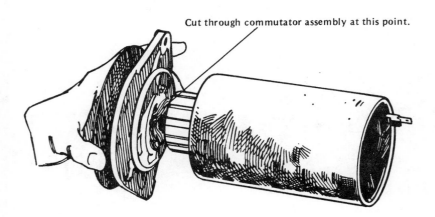

items and secure them with tape or adhesive, making sure
that the pieces of commutator wire are left attached. Do not
contact the items when the unit is reassembled. The brushes
attached to the end plate can be left in place, as no electricity
will be able to pass through the unit with the guts removed.

Alternator disassembly is somewhat more complex, but
as it will not be necessary to reuse the unit once it has been
stripped, the usual care and attention to detail mentioned in
workshop and owner manuals can be ignored. The diagram
below shows the different parts of the alternator, and recommended conversion methods are outlined.

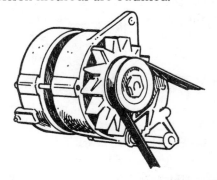

Remove retaining bolts and disassemble front and rear housings. Remove rotor
and replace bearings, spacers, and retainer clips so that the pulley/fan assembly
will still function. Insert items and reassemble housings.

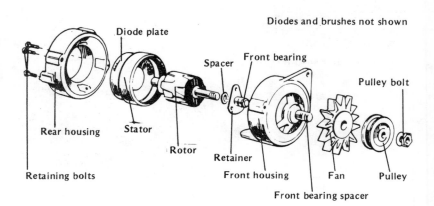

The voltage regulator assembly will obviously not function if the generator or alternator is doctored, and so it is possible to take advantage of the extra space that the removal of this unit's innards will provide. Simply remove the cover of the unit. In some cases this will be factory sealed, and it will be necessary to break a seal to remove the cover, levering or prying it with a screwdriver or knife.

Once the cover is off, two or three coils, or relays, will be visible. Remove these by unscrewing them from the base or by breaking them off if they appear to be molded or welded in place. Insert items and reseal the unit using adhesive, even if the cover was originally only screwed down. Always apply dirt and oil to doctored units to deter close examination.

Voltage regulator box with cover in place

Remove relays for extra space.

Cover removed

Remember that after you have used the above methods your vehicle will have no charging system whatsoever, so it is important that the journey to be undertaken be as short as possible, and that as few of the accessories (lights, wipers, and so on) as possible are used. The ignition warning light will also remain on, and it might be a good idea to remove the bulb from the unit to avoid drawing undue attention.

The vehicle battery itself may also be adapted to conceal items, and the following methods are the simplest and most effective.

Before carrying out the following operation, remove any water that is covering the plates of the battery with a hydrometer or similar tool. With a tank cutter or similar tool cut out a plug from one end of the battery casing. The hole should be made just above the level of the plates and should be of sufficient diameter to allow insertion of the desired items. Battery designs vary, but a hole of about 3/4 inch diameter or slightly more is usually possible. Retain the plug, and using a long drill bit of any large diameter (up to the diameter of the hole) cut through the internal baffles (see diagram). The operation can be done in two stages—one end and then the other—if a very long drill is not available.

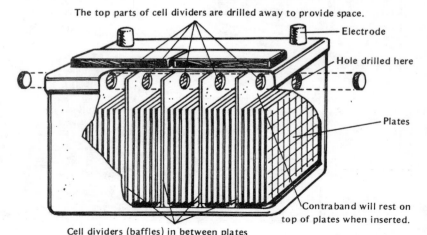

The top parts of cell dividers are drilled away to provide space.

Electrode

Hole drilled here

Plates

Contraband will rest on top of plates when inserted.

Cell dividers (baffles) in between plates

Items to be inserted should be sealed in acid-resistant material, such as pieces cut from rubber gloves. Replace the plug and secure with adhesive, adding a coat of suitable paint or waterproofing material to disguise the plug if necessary. Items can be reclaimed later using long thin tweezers or pliers.

The use of the next method allows you to conceal more, or larger, items. First of all, obtain the smallest battery available that will provide sufficient power for your vehicle's needs. In fact, for your purposes you may only need to start the car once or twice, and in this case a battery of considerably lower power than would normally be fitted would suffice. It should be as small as possible, and to this end I would suggest experimenting with motorcycle and other batteries. Second, obtain the largest possible battery that will fit in the usual position.

Be sure that the battery is completely emptied of water and acid. The best way to do this is to leave the battery turned upside down for a few hours and then flush it out with fresh water. Again, leave it to stand upside down until no more water runs out.

Using a sharp chisel and hammer, split the case of the large battery away from the battery itself. Close examination will reveal the exact position of the join. Look carefully

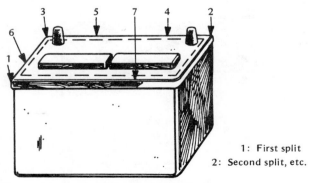

1: First split
2: Second split, etc.

Split the seam along the arrowed lines. Do this carefully, and in stages.

before starting, as design methods vary considerably. Once the seam is split, insert a sharp, long knife or blade between the case and the plates and run it around to free the sides of the case completely.

Turn the battery upside down, and lever out the battery from the case. A few sharp blows on the base of the case will often help speed the process. If difficulty is encountered in removing the plate assembly from the case, bend and break the plates, using pliers or another appropriate tool. Once the assembly is clear of the case, cut the electrodes so as to release the top cover electrodes and battery lugs.

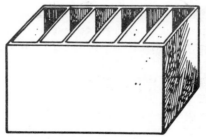

Empty case shell, showing integral cell dividers (baffles)

The next step is to place the small battery inside the case of the large one and pack the items to be hidden around it. Usually, the difference in size between batteries is in the

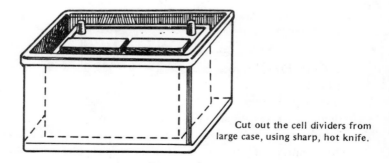

Cut out the cell dividers from large case, using sharp, hot knife.

Cutaway showing small battery in place

length or width, not height. Care must be taken, therefore, to ensure that enough height exists for the cover to be replaced on top of the small battery.

In order that the cables can be connected in a manner that will appear perfectly normal, the electrodes of the small inner battery must be soldered or otherwise attached to the electrodes on the cover. Soldering two lengths of fairly thick, but flexible, wire from electrode to electrode will do the trick. The wires may also be attached by screws. Once the cover is replaced, seal the seam using black putty, mastic, or any black adhesive or putty.

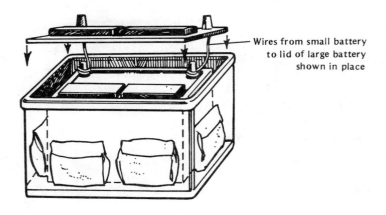

Wires from small battery to lid of large battery shown in place

Small battery in place with contraband packed around it

In *Duty-Free,* in the section covering the conversion of batteries, I mentioned in passing the technique of converting the large, square type of battery into a self-contained explosive device. In response to several requests, the method is shown below.

The beauty of this method is that you end up with a two-in-one situation. The battery, while concealing the explo-

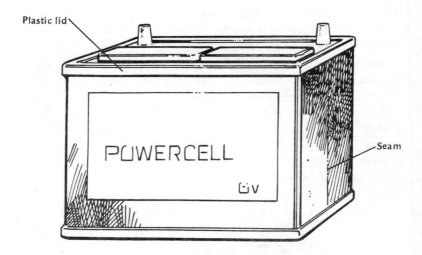

sive, is actually part and parcel of the device itself. The finished item arouses no suspicion, requires little justification in the eyes of border officers, and can be left almost anywhere within the target area.

Locate the seam that holds the metal jacket to the battery. Usually it will be found running down one of the narrower side panels. Pry the seam apart, and gently lever the jacket from around the battery. On the top of the assembly, there will be a plastic lid which holds the connector's terminals. It may be necessary to break the joint between this lid and the battery, but often it can be loosened from the surrounding metal jacket, leaving the card-covered battery and the plastic lid still connected.

With the jacket removed, slice the top quarter from the battery and take a similar slice from the base. Wear gloves and don't pick your nose. The chosen explosive device is assembled, the timer, delay device or other system selected placed on top of the bottom battery slice, and the device packed with suitable items to ensure that the top slice will rest in more or less the correct position. Replace the jacket

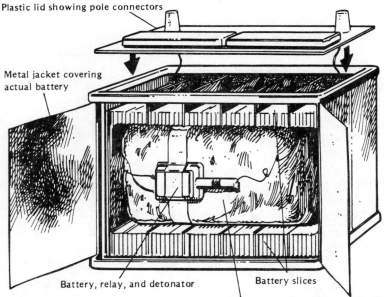

Plastic lid showing pole connectors

Metal jacket covering actual battery

Battery, relay, and detonator

Battery slices

Explosive packed around delay/firing assembly and supporting lid

Seam shown at front for ease of description

and secure the seam using Super Glue. If care is taken not to bend the jacket too much during removal, it will fall back into a tight fit around the innards of the device. A more elaborate method is to construct a small wooden frame to hold the device. The top and bottom slices can then be glued in place and the jacket replaced.

My favorite setup is a battery rundown delay. Use a small transistor radio battery and a relay device of the same voltage. I have found old electro-mechanical pin table machines to be an excellent source of such relays. Experiment with the relay and battery to determine the length of time it takes to run the battery down, buy a new battery, and away you go. For those of you not familiar with such things, the power from the battery holds the relay open. As the battery runs down and eventually dies, the relay contacts close, completing the circuit and detonating the device. From experience, I would say that the safest way of timing the explosion, regardless of what the handbooks say, is that once the device is set, be content to know that it will go off sometime in the near future. Don't rely on any other info being more accurate!

I should make it clear that I am not advocating the indiscriminate distribution of such devices. Bombs are very nasty things and, in their own way, cowardly. The likelihood of killing or maiming an intended victim without hurting anyone else is remote. Almost as remote as you should be when the thing goes off! So, if you must inflict death on others, use decent, moral weapons, like a .38 or a big stick.

On most vehicles the windshield wiper motor assembly is quite large and can easily be adapted to conceal a variety of items. Once again, as designs vary from vehicle to vehicle, it is recommended that you refer to the owner or workshop manual for specific disassembly instructions. However, the diagram below shows a commonly used wiper motor, and the accompanying directions will apply to many different types.

Disassembled Ford Mustang wiper motor

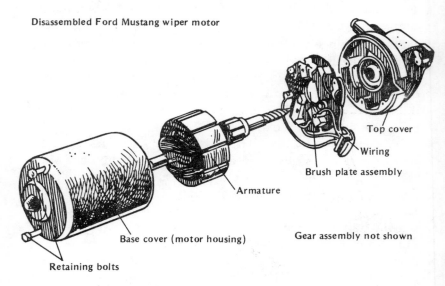

Top cover

Wiring

Brush plate assembly

Armature

Base cover (motor housing)   Gear assembly not shown

Retaining bolts

Contraband inserted in base cover

Having first removed the electrical connections to the unit, unscrew the retaining bolts or screws and remove the base cover (motor housing). Disassemble the armature and brush plate assembly to provide the required space. It will be necessary to cut through the wires that connect the brush plate to the electrical supply. Once this is done, tape the bare wires with electrician's tape as a safety measure. Items can now be inserted and the unit reassembled.

Obviously, the vehicle will now have no wiper system, and therefore care must be taken to avoid using this method during bad weather, not only from a safety point of view, but because inoperative wipers during adverse weather may well attract unwanted attention, even in the form of assistance, during border crossings.

Vehicle gear shifts are easily converted. Most of the types fitted to American and English vehicles have a top which can be unscrewed, and the top itself drilled out to provide a cavity. Alternatively, the shaft itself can be drilled out, and items inserted. Replace the shift lever top with powerful adhesive, and don't overdo the diameter of the hole. Common sense will dictate what size the shaft you are using will receive without becoming too weak.

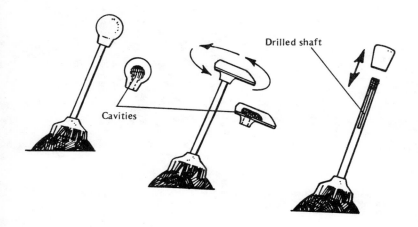

Drilled shaft

Cavities

Many of the older vehicles around have instrument panels from which the speedo, tach, and so on can be removed separately. Check the handbook, though, as many panels are sealed and covered by a single piece of glass. Select the instrument according to ease of disassembly and remove it from the dashboard. Most of the speedos I have removed and adapted have been held together by a simple collar band (see below). Once this is removed, the glass and face of the speedo can be lifted out and access gained to the inside of the unit. There is usually plenty of space available and, providing the unit is reassembled carefully and replaced in the dash without undue scratching and damage to the fascia, it will remain undetectable.

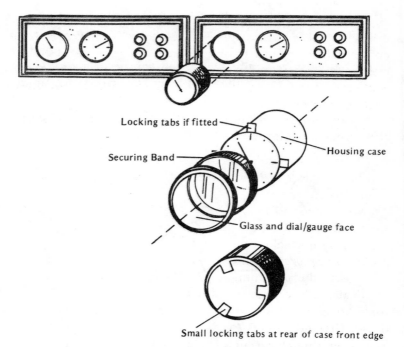

Locking tabs if fitted

Securing Band

Housing case

Glass and dial/gauge face

Small locking tabs at rear of case front edge

Some gauges are fastened to the housing case with small tubes which may be bent back to obtain access.

2.
SECURITY
EVASION
HIDES

THIS CHAPTER IS APPLICABLE TO those instances where, for various reasons, goods must be conveyed across borders or into secure areas without the formality of customs clearance or other scrutiny, and when it is desired that the crossing itself be made without the knowledge of government authorities.

Most border control techniques employed by different governments fall into three categories:

1. *Border observation or surveillance,* in which static and mobile guards or observers monitor the border area on a regular basis;

2. *Border closure,* in which physical barriers are erected the length and breadth of the border, effectively preventing a crossing by normal means; and

3. *Border ignorance,* in which, although a border does actually exist, the government of the country or state finds it politically advantageous to ignore its existence, and to enforce its purpose only when external pressure forces it to do so. (Ireland ignores the border of Northern Ireland in this way, even though certain people would deny the fact!)

If you intend to use the following methods, plan your route carefully. You may find that, as is usually the case, it is easier to go around certain countries or areas than through them, and it is always better to be a few weeks late with a delivery than to be prevented from making it at all! The main ingredient for successful operations of this type is detailed study and analysis of the obstacles in your path.

The first thing to do is obtain suitable equipment with which to monitor the radio frequencies used by the guards, border authorities, and so on. Keep a detailed record of the coming and going of patrols, numbers involved, type of transport used, and other relevant information. Once a pattern emerges, and you are as sure as you can be of the official patrol schedule, it is time to make your move.

At this point, two completely separate sets of plans must be made. One will be the genuine operation, in which items, personnel, or whatever are to be transported across the border. The other will be a decoy, the purpose of which will be not only to distract attention from the early stages of the "real thing," but also to ensure that a disproportionate number of border officials are compelled to investigate the decoy, thereby preventing their interference with the actual crossing, even if it becomes apparent that it is taking place.

For the sake of example, we will imagine that the border to be crossed is situated inland, and that the position of crossing has been selected to take advantage of natural cover—hilly, woodland country—in which it is impractical for authorities to erect effective physical barriers. The crossing will take place at night, preferably under bad weather conditions, as both these factors will help immeasurably to make the operation a success. The number of officials on call has been determined by monitoring the radio traffic and other surveillance, and your team has sufficient personnel to outnumber them by at least 1.5 to 1. For the sake of argument we will say that you have determined the number of personnel required to be 15. They will be divided into three groups: the runners, who will convey the contraband to the border perimeter, and actually make the crossing when the time comes; and two squads of blockers, who will create any necessary diversion and effectively prevent any interference with the crossing.

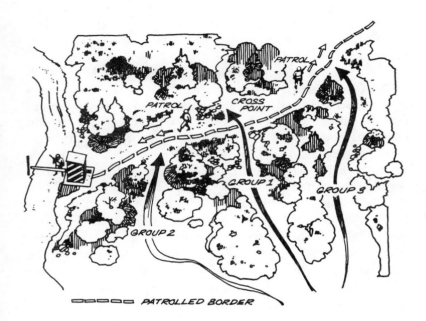

The three groups move toward the border perimeter in the manner shown above. If either group of blockers suspects that border security personnel has noticed signs of covert activity, either through intercepted radio traffic or due to unusual movement by the guards, they begin diversionary activities—"over the top" behavior designed to attract attention—such as the flashing of colored signal lamps, the shouting of instructions, and so on.

Under cover of this activity, the runner group makes the crossing and continues to "safety," a prearranged pick-up point manned by persons with a sound knowledge of the area, and with suitable alibis for all members of the team.

After a suitable length of time the blockers disperse and leave the area as best they can.

It is best to use expendable personnel as blockers, as it is quite usual for at least some of them to be caught. Pay them in advance for their services, and make sure that they do not have any incriminating information about you or the main team.

There are obviously a lot of variables involved here, such as the precise nature of the border, the value of the items that are being moved, and the relationship between the countries on either side of the border. Nevertheless, the general principles apply. In most of the operations of this nature that I have known about, firearms have been carried by members of the blocking teams; and it cannot be denied that this gives one a definite edge.

When the border in question takes the form of a physical barrier, barbed wire fencing or a concrete wall, for example, the major problem is determining whether or not the barrier can be breached in the first place, and if so, whether it can be done without attracting attention. In most cases the answer to question one will be yes; the answer to question two is invariably no. Once again some form of diversion is needed, but it is likely that such a diversion as mentioned earlier would be insufficient to enable the breaching of any elaborate defenses. That being the case, not only would the intended crossing have to be aborted, but the resultant panic would have the effect of drastically increasing security in the future. The following example of how to overcome such situations should give you a few ideas.

As in the first example, the behavior and methods of the border patrol must be observed for sufficient time to enable a prediction chart to be drawn up, so that the position of the guards in relation to the border at any given time can be reliably estimated.

Reconnoiter the place of crossing to determine what equipment will be required to breach it. Take care also to search for any alarm systems that may be present.

Over a period of time, convey the required tools and equipment to the border perimeter, evading patrols by constant reference to the prediction chart. Watch continually for any change in the patrol routines, and update the chart accordingly. Operate under cover of darkness whenever possible and take advantage of bad weather.

Begin to disassemble the barrier gradually, using a small alarm watch or timer to ensure that the work time spent at the barrier does not exceed a safe limit. Shortly before the next patrol is expected, reassemble the dismantled barrier, secrete the tools, and then either hide or leave the area. Obviously, the barrier need not be reassembled properly, just enough to give the impression that it has not been tampered with. If the barrier is of too solid a design to be disassembled by hand, use this preliminary period to plant explosive charges.

When the barrier is sufficiently disassembled to facilitate its swift removal—or destruction—hire a couple more helpers for added security and have them attempt to cross at points that will not jeopardize your own crossing. Then make your move. If all has gone well, the time saved by your preliminary work will not only make the crossing possible, but positively easy.

If it is possible to dismantle the barrier rather than destroy it, it is a good idea to have a partner accompany you to the crossing and rebuild the barrier once you are through. In this way the crossing point may be used more than once. If this method is used, do not employ decoys. A word of caution though: If you come across one of these "doors," ignore it and make your own. Many known crossing sites are left unrepaired in order that careless users will walk straight into the arms of waiting security personnel.

It is taken for granted that you will have arranged a reception committee to meet you on the other side, and that the helpers you have employed know nothing of the real plan.

Remember that in all of these operations contact with the border security personnel should be avoided. On many occasions, it will be found that it is possible to make a crossing without the need for diversionary tactics. It is better, however, to have them arranged and not need them than to make the crossing without support.

Should the situation arise where you find your intended route blocked or patrolled by dogs without handlers, as at a very well-known border where the dogs are loose-chained to a run wire which enables them to guard a given area without being able to wander off or be lured away, there are a few things you can do to divert their attention. The least favored requires considerable nerve and involves luring the dog toward oneself, and then overpowering it SAS style. It is more likely that the overpowering would consist of spraying powerful poison, or acid, or any other incapacitating substance into the animal's face. Alternatives are shooting (use a silenced weapon), stabbing (wear thick gloves), or running (my favorite).

The use of bitches to lure the dogs away from the crossing point is often effective, but about the most realistic method I have come across is to use a tape recording of an animal of the same breed as those employed as guard dogs uttering sounds of distress. How you obtain these recordings is up to you, but I have never known it to fail. Have the recording start and stop at random, and place the machine, which will obviously be small, self-contained and well camouflaged, well away from your intended crossing point.

Another method is to closely monitor the actions of the border staff when they call the animals for feeding. Try to learn what commands the animals respond to. With the wealth of sophisticated surveillance equipment on the market nowadays, it shouldn't be too hard to obtain recordings of the actual commands given!

Equally ferocious dogs with terrible temperaments could be trained and released into the patrol path of those on the border. Also food, well dosed with poison, has been used often and with much success. Always remember, however, if evasion can be achieved, it is obviously preferable to confrontation.

Borders that are too long for a regular patrol to keep secure with enough success to warrant the manpower required are often mined. Should you come across such an area which must be crossed, the following tips should help.

First choice is the use of a dog which is sent out across the suspect area. If it makes it across, follow the route it took exactly. Obviously the average dog weighs considerably less than an adult human, so load the animal with a belt or yoke attachment holding sufficient weight to approximate the poundage of the heaviest person that will cross. Depending on terrain and location, other animals may be available. I have recently returned from a short trip to visit a few friends where, owing to the political situation, large areas, especially those on or near the borders, have been mined. These particular anti-personnel mines are nasty little affairs that resemble the rocks strewn around the area. They explode on contact, and the only way I would agree to travel the route chosen by my hosts was if the donkeys that were carrying most of the luggage, so to speak, were led in front, with me following very closely in their footsteps, or hoof steps if you prefer. I was subjected to considerable ribbing, but it didn't bother me one bit.

Should the area to be crossed be quite narrow, and you can't afford bangalore torpedos, obtain several heavy, long pieces of wood or piping. Hurl these out into the intended crossing area as shown below. Assuming the planks don't explode and kill you with bits of shrapnel, it should be OK to walk the plank, throwing out more lengths as you proceed across the area. Where possible, get someone else to do this for you! The rewards for such risks would have to be considerable, of course, but if you are prepared and able to undertake such operations, there are plenty of people willing and ready to foot the bill.

A considerable number of borders take the form of rivers or lakes, and several countries have exposed coastlines or coastal rivers. It is impossible for these locations to be secured against illegal crossing or infiltration, other than by relatively simple patrol techniques. The following section shows how to successfully breach such defenses, but make sure that you have adequate intelligence about the number and components of the security personnel guarding or patrolling the area, a prediction chart and list of their radio frequencies, call signs, and so on, before commencing the crossing.

The type of vessel used will obviously be determined by the nature of the water to be crossed. In any case, remember to thoroughly waterproof the items to be moved. (See Chapter 5.)

For river crossings, either coastal or inland, I recommend the method shown below.

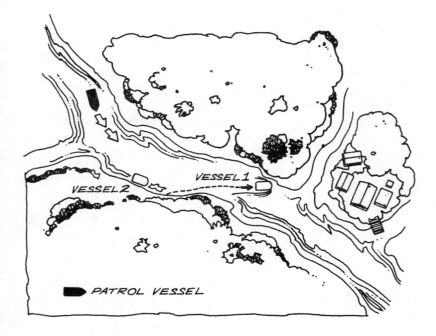

Enlist a group of helpers to assist you in carrying out the operation. You must determine how many helpers you will need, taking into account the type and amount of contraband you are moving and other considerations of your individual enterprise. The group is divided into two teams, each traveling in a separate vessel. The first contains only expendable personnel, no contraband—although, of course, they think that they *do* have contraband! The second contains more personnel and the items to be moved. Vessel one moves out towards the border at a suitable time, as determined by the prediction chart, under cover of vessel two.

If vessel one is intercepted or its position detected by security forces, the team in vessel two abort the operation and clear the area. It is important that the team in vessel one believe that you and the rest of team two will come to their aid if any such difficulty is encountered, but it would be foolish for you to do so. (Make sure you pay them in advance!)

If all appears to be going well, vessel two makes its way across towards the border, under cover of team one. If it is necessary to breach some form of physical barrier, have team one operate in obviously detectable locations, while your team crosses at a more suitable point unlikely to be discovered before that of the other team.

Alternative decoy methods that have been used successfully are the sending across of unmanned small vessels to coincide with the actual crossing, and the placing of obstacles along the known patrol route of the security forces. Anchored marker buoys may be used, planted in such a manner as to be noticeable but not too obvious. Make sure that the time involved in removing and investigating the decoys will delay the patrol for a sufficient length of time to allow a crossing to be made. The decoys could take the form of large, sealed metal boxes containing replica weapons, white powder, and so on. Secure the boxes to a length of chain or rope and affix this to a homemade marker buoy (a plastic can will

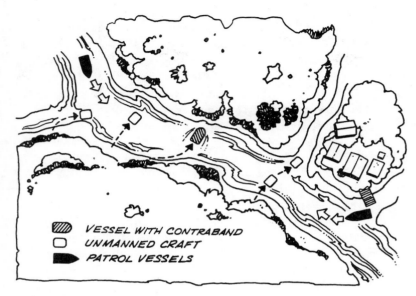

VESSEL WITH CONTRABAND
UNMANNED CRAFT
PATROL VESSELS

do). Paint or mark the boxes with fake coded identification figures—utter rubbish—as this will encourage suspicion by the crew of the craft that discovers them.

VESSEL WITH CONTRABAND
MARKER BUOYS
PATROL VESSELS

The use of lightweight inflatable craft is recommended, as these vessels can be easily disposed of—deflated and buried, for example—once the crossing is made. Always try to make water-based crossings under cover of bad weather and darkness. Use reception committees whenever possible, both to speed the process of clearing the area once the crossing is made, and to help with diversions if necessary.

3.
IMPROVISED
LANDING STRIPS

Various situations call for the use of an airborne crossing, usually when the items to be moved are of sufficient value to justify the costs involved, or when the border to be crossed is so well guarded or inaccessible by normal methods that aircraft are the only way open. When the cash is available, an airborne crossing is by far the simplest to achieve with total success.

Obviously, to land legally in a foreign country, you must let the authorities know of the fact, and allow the aircraft to be searched according to the customs laws applicable at the time. This kind of welcome may defeat your purposes, however, and is easily avoided by using the following techniques.

The simplest and most popular method is to "crash" the aircraft under cover of darkness at a prearranged point, and leave the area with a reception committee. For this type of operation, the committee will consist of enough personnel and transportation to unload and convey to safety the articles in question, and at least one person trained and equipped to deal with simple medical emergencies that may result from the "crash." By *crash* I do not mean a completely uncontrolled emergency landing, but rather a landing on highly unsuitable terrain that is very likely to damage the aircraft beyond repair, or where it will be impossible for other reasons to take off in the aircraft again once it is down. Examples are hastily cleared woodland, areas surrounded by high trees or other obstacles, and marshy, swampy terrain.

If the area to be used as a crash strip is prepared a considerable time before use, take care to disguise any clearing work so as to avoid easy detection by security patrols. Marker lights, if used, should not be switched on (or lit if using the fire-bucket type of marker) until shortly before the aircraft's arrival. A suggested layout for a crash strip, indicating the position of lights and so on, is shown below.

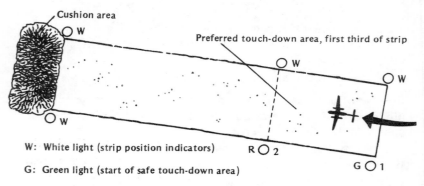

W: White light (strip position indicators)

G: Green light (start of safe touch-down area)

R: Red light (end of safe touch-down area; if touch-down is not made before this point, the aircraft cannot land safely)

The colors of the lights are not critical, so long as their meaning is understood by the pilot. However, it is important that lights 1 and 2 be different. In daylight, colored panels or smoke can be used instead of lights.

For a crash strip, surface preparation can be limited to the removal of any very large obstructions, such as rocks larger than a football, and so on; it is not necessary to create a perfectly flat surface. Bushes, long, thick grass and any other soft obstacles that are removed should be placed in the cushion area, and any available firefighting equipment should be close to this point also. Specific dimensions for the strip will depend upon the aircraft used, and this information should be obtained from the pilot. The minimum safe distances required for landing and takeoff under various conditions will be contained in the aircraft operator's manual.

However, as a general guideline a runway 800 feet long and 40 feet wide, at minimum, will safely accommodate most commonly used light aircraft on daylight operations, in a moderate to hot climate, and where the area to be used as a landing strip is less than 1000 meters above sea level. For night operations, the minimum width of the runway should be 100 feet. If the area of operation has temperatures of over thirty-eight degrees centigrade, 20 percent should be added to the length of the strip; and if the area is more than 1000 meters above sea level, add 10 percent to the strip's length for each 300 meters of extra altitude. This allows for the decreased air density that occurs under such conditions.

Although the dimensions herein are refered to as minimum dimensions, it will be found that under certain conditions and with certain aircraft the necessary length and width of the strip will be somewhat less than stated. This is because I have deliberately allowed for a degree of extra safety and variations in pilot experience.

According to the book, all landings and takeoffs should be made into the wind; for our purposes, designing a strip along such lines is not practical, and the strip should therefore be positioned so that any prevailing wind will aid either the landing or takeoff. (Discuss this with the pilot.)

For a strip capable of providing safe, regular landing and takeoff facilities, more attention must be paid to the surface preparation. As well as clearing obvious hazards, and ensuring that the surface is not deeply rutted or overly soft, strong grass over two feet in height should be removed and, if possible, small stones strewn over the surface. An extra safety area should be cleared at each end of the runway, and along the sides of the strip. Ten- to twenty-foot-wide strips should be cleared to crash strip standards along the sides, and a similar distance at the top and bottom. Also, additional strip markers should be used to indicate the full dimensions of the strip to make things that much easier for the pilot. The "lightstick" type of luminous plastic tubes are ideal for this purpose. Space them out along the perimeter of the basic runway, that is, inside the safety areas.

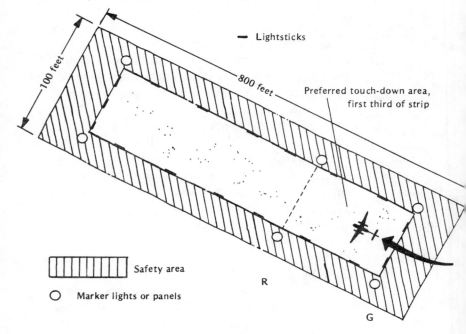

Once again, the precise dimensions of the strip will depend upon the aircraft in question. The diagram above shows a strip suitable for the landing and takeoff of most light aircraft under night conditions, and these are the minimum dimensions that should be used for such operations (unless you really dislike the pilot!).

The strip surface itself should be cleared to a higher standard than that of the crash strip, and the ground should not be too soft or deeply rutted. The easiest method for determining the suitability of the surface is to drive a vehicle along it at high speed. If the vehicle does not catch on the surface and finish the run in a battered heap, it should be OK. An unusually soft surface can be packed down by driving the vehicle along it repeatedly.

While the location of the strip should be chosen to take advantage of any natural cover, care must be taken to ensure that the runway area is not too heavily fenced in by surrounding obstacles such as tall trees. As can be seen from the diagram below, fixed wing aircraft will be unable to drop vertically onto the runway (unless you have access to a Harrier), and therefore a relatively clear glide path must be provided for the plane to follow down onto the strip. Ascertain from the pilot the glide/climb characteristics of the aircraft to be used and remove or otherwise alter nearby hazards accordingly.

The following diagram shows the relevant distances involved for a light aircraft capable of taking off, or gliding in, within the following ratio: One foot of height gained or lost for every twenty feet of horizontal distance traveled. This is expressed as a 1:20 glide/climb ratio.

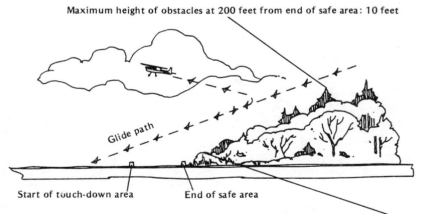

Maximum height of obstacles at 200 feet from end of safe area: 10 feet

Glide path

Start of touch-down area   End of safe area

Maximum height of obstacles at 80 feet from end of safe area: 4 feet

Note how the aircraft turns back on itself after takeoff, thereby taking advantage of the cleared area to gain extra height. If you intend to use the strip on several occasions, take care to provide adequate camouflage from ground or air patrols that may be operating in the area. Of course, it is only a matter of time before the authorities catch on to the fact that the area is being used for covert landing operations, but you can buy yourself a little more of the valuable commodity by disguising the strip's exact whereabouts as skillfully as possible.

First choice for this sort of work has to be the camouflage netting material that is available from most military surplus outlets. Obtain long, wide rolls of the netting, and attach pieces of genuine foliage and leaves for a more realistic appearance. (If the strip is located in an unwooded area, forget the leaves!) These mats can be used to cover the entire runway until shortly before it is needed, at which time they can be simply rolled back out of the way.

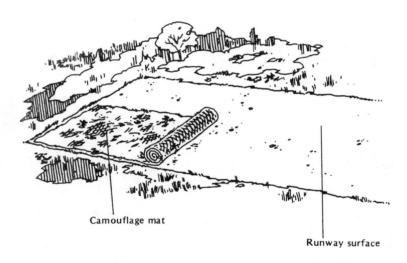

Camouflage mat

Runway surface

As regards the removal of trees and other obstacles for glide path purposes, instead of simply cutting them down and thereby making the strip area highly visible, use the *break-neck* technique. This technique can be used on small- to medium-sized trees or bushes with great effect. It involves

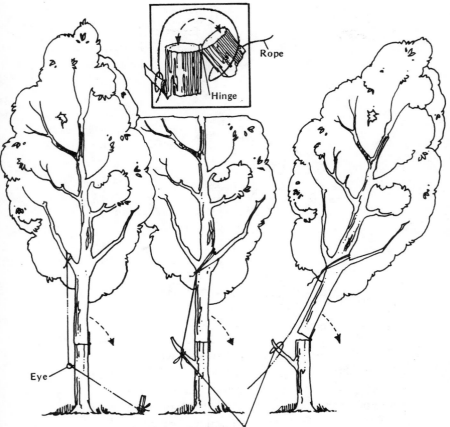

Free end of rope can be secured around branch instead of eye.

cutting off the portion of tree to be removed and then attaching a form of hinge and hook-and-eye contrivance. The idea is that the top part of the tree can be lowered to allow safe access for the incoming aircraft, and then hoisted back into place when the operation is over. The effect is an apparently undisturbed treeline which would otherwise give the strip location away once a patrol got close. I have found that when large, heavy trees are involved it is easier to attach the hinge before cutting through the tree.

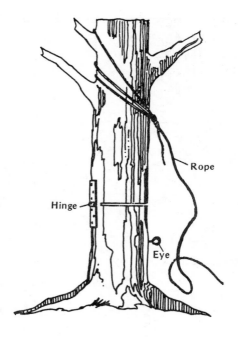

Until quite recently, it would have been highly unlikely for any but the most elaborately backed smuggling operations to have had access to helicopters. However, the last few years have seen the rapid growth of the mini-copter or gyro-copter aircraft industry, and many variations on these tiny choppers are now readily, and relatively cheaply, available. The following section applies to both these minis and their full-sized brothers (just in case you ever get into the big time!).

As these rotary-winged aircraft can land and take off almost vertically, the preparation of a suitable strip (in this case it is actually a pad) is greatly simplified. In fact, providing there is enough room for the rotor blades, a pad just slightly larger than the dimensions of the landing gear will suffice. The pad should be as flat as possible, but in any case should have no more than a 15 percent gradient. Once again, specific dimensions will be determined by the size of the 'copter, but the diagram below shows the manner in which the pad should be constructed.

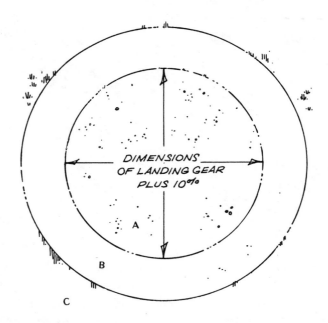

DIMENSIONS OF LANDING GEAR PLUS 10%

A: Flattened, cleared area of a size 10 percent greater than the size of the helicopter landing gear

B: 15-foot-wide safety area cleared to within half the height of the rotors

C: As much of the surrounding area cleared of hazards and debris as is practical

If the ground on which the pad is to be constructed is very dusty or is covered with leaves or other debris, the downdraft of the rotors will create a mini hurricane, and pilot visibility may well be impaired dangerously. To avoid this always ensure that the ground is cleared of loose debris, or, if dusty, wetted down prior to the craft's arrival.

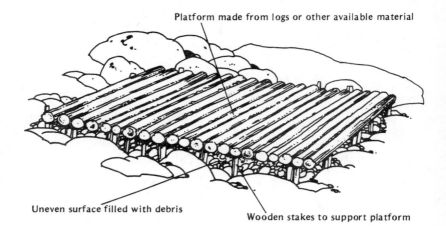

Platform made from logs or other available material

Uneven surface filled with debris

Wooden stakes to support platform

Should the ground be very soft or uneven, it will be best to build some form of platform capable of withstanding the weight of the 'copter. A suitable platform is shown above, the size of which should be the same as that of the landing gear on the 'copter to be used, plus six feet on all sides for safety.

The principle of marking the pad is the same as for rigid-winged aircraft: lights to indicate the position of the landing area itself, and the preferred (safest) touchdown point within that area. As helicopters are much more susceptible to gusting or strong winds, the pad lights must also indicate the direction of the wind.

The lights or panels used can be any available color. The four lights making the square indicate the touchdown area, and the two lights together at the top of the pad indicate the wind direction, enabling the pilot to land into the wind.

Nearby hazards that are likely to interfere with the approach or takeoff should be removed according to the glide/climb information obtained from the pilot.

Some of the very small rotary-winged aircraft available are more suited for use with a fixed-wing type of airstrip as

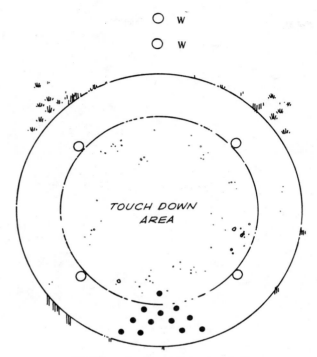

Direction of approach (into the wind)

Wind direction lights should be different colors or sufficiently distances from each other to be obvious.

they have poor glide/climb ratios and require a considerable amount of runway before being able to lift off.

4.
AIR DROP TECHNIQUES

In MANY INSTANCES, DUE TO lack of finance, lack of personnel, or a multitude of other problems that cannot be easily overcome, it will not be possible to use a landing strip for covert air delivery. In such circumstances, or whenever an aircraft is available but you do not want to make a landing, airdrop methods can be used.

The main physical problem with such techniques has always been positioning, or more specifically, being able to predict exactly where articles will land once they are jettisoned from the aircraft. On more than one occasion I have been witness to the sickening (but quite funny) sight of deliveries intended for our group drifting away into the distance never to be seen again! The following techniques should help overcome any such difficulties.

First, select the drop zone carefully. It should be as flat as possible, bearing in mind the recovery of the items, and yet should provide sufficient concealment from any police, border guards, and so on.

If the drop is to take place during daylight, wait until dark before leaving the area. In either case, always have a decoy team in the area. The job of the decoy team will be to bait any patrols that threaten to interfere with the operation. They should leave the drop area slightly ahead of the recovery team. Once an area is selected, it should be marked as shown below.

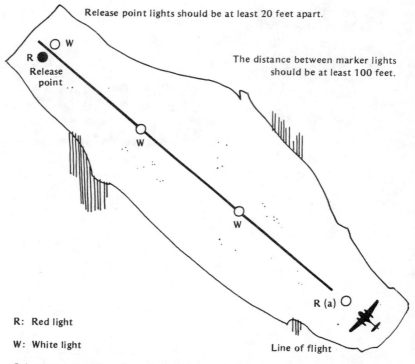

Release point lights should be at least 20 feet apart.

The distance between marker lights should be at least 100 feet.

R: Red light

W: White light

Line of flight

Colors are not critical, but release point markers should consist of two different colors.

The aircraft that is to make the drop is flown into a general prearranged area, and the pilot and crewmember look for the marker lights. Once these are found, the pilot positions the aircraft so as to fly along the line of lights. The first light (a) indicates the start of the drop area. The second and third lights are markers indicating the line of flight, and the final two lights (side by side) indicate the desired drop position. It is over these last two lights that the articles will be ejected. The ground team members must position themselves so as to be able to quickly and easily recover the items once they have landed. The position of the ground team will be based on the following factors:

- Whether the items are to fall free or by parachute.
- The dispersion area, if more than one item is dropped. (Dispersion area is the distance between the first and the last article once they have hit the ground.)
- The forward-throw effect. (Forward throw is the distance that the item will travel horizontally after it has been jettisoned from the aircraft and before the parachute opens.)

The aircraft making the drop must be flown at a pre-arranged height and speed so that the ground team can correctly predict the likely impact point or points of the items. Obviously, minor variations will be inevitable.

For drops using a parachute, calculate impact point as follows:

Dispersion (in meters) = half aircraft speed (in knots) x exit time (in seconds).

(Exit time is the elapsed time between the exits of the first and the last package from the aircraft.)

Wind drift (in meters) = aircraft height (in hundreds of feet) x wind speed (in knots) x the constant, 3.

(Wind drift is the distance to one side of the aircraft's line of flight that the package or packages dropped will travel, due to prevailing wind conditions.)

To determine forward throw factor for drops with parachute, move the release point marker 100 meters towards the aircraft's approach direction (that is, 100 meters *away* from the desired impact point, in the direction of the approaching aircraft).

For drops without a parachute, wind speed and drift are ignored. Dispersion is calculated as for drops with a parachute, and forward throw compensation is achieved by moving the release point marker *away* from the desired impact point, in the direction of the approaching aircraft, a distance roughly equal to the altitude of the aircraft.

The diagram below shows the positions of the release point markers and the ground recovery team in relation to the overall drop area.

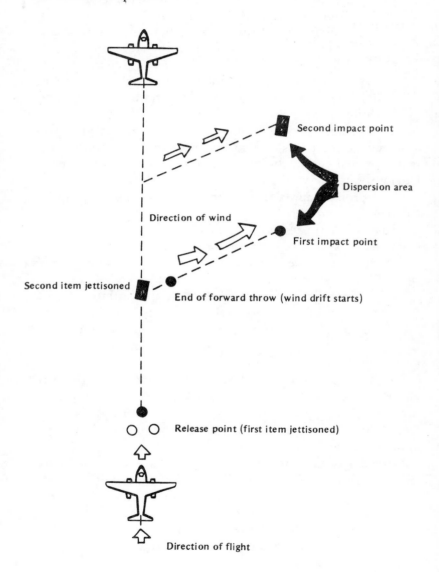

Under certain circumstances it may be possible to arrange a drop into a given location without the need for markers or elaborate planning. The drop may be made from a very low flying aircraft (the techniques mentioned in this chapter are applicable to drops made from no more than 700 feet) such as a "hedge hopping" light plane or 'copter. Also, items can be dropped into coastal waters (where a reception team will be waiting) by aircraft that will be landing, perfectly legally, on a regular strip further inland.

5.
WORDS
TO THE WISE

DESPITE THE COMPLEXITY OF SOME of the techniques shown herein, my advice is to keep any operation you undertake as simple as possible. Prepare for an elaborate military style crossing by all means, but if it becomes apparent that simply walking through will suffice, do just that. Although the elaborate, multipersonnel operations generally have a higher success rate than unsupported ones, they also have an inherent danger, namely the personnel themselves. Although I hate to say it, for every other person involved with an op, your chances of discovery or failure increase accordingly.

Always use the "need to know" method when recruiting or briefing personnel, and pay at least a large percentage of the wages up front to encourage loyalty in team members. When using helpers as part of a decoy team, it is important that they believe themselves to be the heart of the operation (this is where the "need to know" technique comes in). In the early stages of an operation, always try to feed team members that you do not know well with misinformation. This will quickly show up any leaks you have, and, providing you tread carefully, will add greatly to the success of the op. Many customs agents and other officials operate on a sort of freelance basis, and often it is these special operatives that actually sow the seeds for an operation in the first place. This is illegal in most countries; it is, in fact, entrapment. However, as with all these things, the law is on their side unless they are caught, or entrapment can be proven against them. The bottom line, then, is that if you suspect someone of being a plant, use him to throw a screen around the real op by feeding him with the wrong dates, wrong location, and other misleading information.

Every now and then a situation will arise where in order to be inconspicuous one has to be very, very obvious! For example, what could be less suspicious around a border area than border guards? Get the idea? Believe me, in all but the smallest of border areas or secure areas, the guards or officers on duty will personally know only a handful of the other guards. Providing that someone is wearing the correct uniform, has the correct manner, and carries I.D. to support the masquerade, then that someone will be able to pass quite easily through the area.

Those of you reading this who have had military or security experience might like to think back to those occasions when you saluted a superior officer or maybe exchanged a few pleasantries without having had any *real* proof as to his identity, save for his uniform and manner; I would be very surprised to hear that you have never had this experience.

With this in mind, have someone monitor the border or area for a few months to see if any new personnel are posted in. These rookies are always the best bet for bulling.

The problems that "sniffer" dogs can cause were mentioned earlier in this book, so here is a way to get through such checks without any big problems. Obviously, the main problem with conveying items or substances that have a powerful odor is that in order to mask the smell one usually has to use another strong-smelling substance. This "secondary aroma" leads the canine to the contraband. The sniffer dogs that I have come across have either been trained to recognize specific substances such as drugs and explosives, or to sniff out any item that smells out of place, like gun oil in a bag of potatoes. One well-used substance for distinguishing the odor of certain drugs is talcum powder, either scented, providing it would not appear (sorry, smell) out of place, or unscented. Talc has the effect of absorbing certain odors and, along with simple air fresheners, can be effective in some circumstances. In all honesty though, the above are, at best, little better than nothing. The real thing is G.A.C. (granular activated charcoal). This substance, obtainable from any pharmacy, will effectively eliminate even the strongest of odors, and yet has little or no smell itself. I could list a few occasions on which G.A.C. has fooled sniffer dogs, but the information might tend to incriminate me as the contraband that the animals overlooked—or oversmelled—was in fact high explosive. The best way to use G.A.C. is to seal the contraband item or substance in a plastic bag, seal it, and then place that bag inside another containing the charcoal, seal well, and conceal.

Contraband inside plastic bag

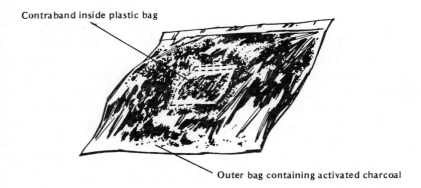

Outer bag containing activated charcoal

A word or two about places of concealment is in order here, I think. No doubt a few of you have noticed that some of the hides in this and the preceding book will conceal only small items, or items in small quantities. The thing to remember, however, is that if you multiply the hides, increasing the number of specific hide types in use at one time, larger quantities can be carried. A good example is the toothpaste tube; on its own it will enable you to move contraband in personal quantities, but if you were to import, as part of a business operation, several boxes of toothpaste—well, I'm sure you get the picture.

Ostensibly legal imports and exports of all kinds of goods and equipment are used every day to convey contraband. As in the case of personal imports, the customs authorities cannot afford the time to check every crate or container. In fact, six times out of ten, the only proof of what is actually inside a crate is the shipping declaration/manifest that is attached to the article. A recent incident in the United States publicized this fact quite well, much to the embarrassment of the government. An attempt was made to smuggle a very valuable piece of equipment out of the United States and into the hands of the Russians. The equipment was a restricted item used for the manufacture of "chips" (I.C.s). Fortunately, a spot check revealed that the crate labelled "machine parts" or something equally as stupid actually contained this million dollar goody. What devious, Connor type of method had been used to disguise the unique piece of equipment? Had it been fitted into a dummy exterior that fit the bill? Actually, no, nothing whatsoever had been done to disguise the unit. The multimillion dollar espionage/smuggling ring was so confident the crate wouldn't be opened they didn't bother. It just shows how blasé even the professionals can get!

As it turned out, the espionage/smuggling ring was busted because the customs agents let the crate (but not its contents) continue on its merry way, leading them to all the members of the team. The moral of this story is simply that if you're going to do something, do it properly. Don't get me wrong—my advice applies to customs authorities as well as to would-be smugglers.

The vehicular hides in this book and *Duty-Free* apply equally to most other forms of transport, aircraft, yachts, and so on. Many fine hides can be found in tubular handrails, cable ducts, and other unlikely places. Once again, the list of this type of hide is endless.

Those of you who have some form of crossing in mind, but are a bit short of cash on hand, might consider the use of radio-controlled aircraft as a replacement for the real thing! It will be quite difficult to find someone small enough to act as a crewmember for airdrop ops, but a possible technique could go something like this: A suitably sized aircraft is obtained along with two identical control units. Operator 1 flies the loaded aircraft across the border from a safe location. At the halfway point, operator 2 takes control of the plane. Sounds quite good, I might even try that one myself! I think that the speed of the aircraft and the distances involved would make it impossible for an unprepared border authority to react quickly enough to stop the op, even if he realized what was going on.

A more elaborate technique would be to employ two identical aircraft. As the delivery craft arrives, the second plane is flown out, giving the impression to anyone watching that it was the same plane returning. It might be a good idea to enlist the aid of a youngster to fly the plane so that if suspicion is aroused and some sort of patrol is sent to investigate, the youngster can apologize profusely and get nothing more than a scolding from the security personnel for playing near a restricted area.

To conclude, it's worth remembering that, should you have to cross some form of restricted area covertly, it is usually better to run, or at least move briskly, than to adopt a cautious, military style of movement. The reason for this is that the sudden command, "Halt, security forces," has the effect of making a walking man stop. You will also find it difficult to suddenly break into a run under such conditions. The effect of the same unexpected command on a runner is exactly the opposite: that is to say, he or she will run faster. Of course it's "horses for courses" here. If running will attract attention that would not otherwise be drawn, you won't run, will you?

In preparing this book and *Duty-Free,* I have endeavored to illustrate hides and techniques that I feel are equally useful to the average guy in the street who, for reasons of his own, wishes to avoid paying duty on certain items, and to the professional who hopes to convey items of sufficient value to justify the risk involved, and may be working freelance or for an employer. I have deliberately avoided duplicating places of concealment, as it is quite obvious that the technique for doctoring a football can also be applied to a tennis ball, and so on. There is no need to relist all the stages of conversion. Although drugs and firearms spring readily to mind when one hears mention of smuggling, it should be remembered that fat profits, or a desire to avoid paying in duty what one had saved in purchase cost, are not the only incentives to the smuggler.

If you are at loose ends, independently wealthy, and in search of excitement, why not try the following little test. Using the techniques in this book and *Duty-Free,* convey two packages to central Poland, one of the packages containing assorted weaponry, and the other assorted groceries (fresh meat, toothpaste, chocolate. Oh, yes; and a couple of pairs of Levi jeans!). Put the word around that you have certain items for sale, and wait to see which of the packages brings in the highest bid. You might be very surprised!

Believe it or not, Bibles and foodstuffs are more frequently smuggled into certain countries than firearms or dope. Remember, in certain countries outside of the free West, many items that are everyday and commonplace to you and me are illegal, prohibited, or just not available. It wasn't all that long ago that contraceptives were a prohibited import in Ireland (Eire), and I know for a fact that in the year immediately preceding the lifting of the ban, more money was made smuggling rubbers than revolvers! Just think about that for a moment. If *you* were caught smuggling them, how the hell could you explain away 500 packages of Trojans?

At this point, I think I should give you the professional's definition of a professional, as the word pertains to smuggling. Quite simply, the professional smuggler is the guy who hasn't been caught—*yet!*

A final word about the hides in these books; some are quite simple, and are intended to withstand only cursory examination. Others are more reliable when you are playing the game for high stakes; and several are the kind of place you wish you'd used when you get caught using the other two! Seriously though, always remember that while customs officers and border guards are not infallible, they are not stupid either. Use a cache that fits the bill, and you will be surprised just what you can get away with—*Duty-Free*.